DATA LITERACY IN THE REAL WORLD:
Conversations & Case Studies

EDITED BY

Kristin Fontichiaro   Amy Lennex
Tyler Hoff   Kelly Hovinga   Jo Angela Oehrli

Each piece in this document is Copyright © 2017 by the author named in the piece. Some rights reserved. Each piece is licensed under the Creative Commons Attribution-NonCommercial-ShareAlike 4.0 International Public License. To view a copy of this license, visit http://creativecommons.org/licenses/by-nc-sa/4.0/ or send a letter to Creative Commons, PO Box 1866, Mountain View, California, 94042, USA.

This project was made possible in part by the Institute of Museum and Library Services RE-00-15-0113-15, the University of Michigan School of Information, and the University of Michigan Library.

Published in the United States of America by
Michigan Publishing
Manufactured in the United States of America

DOI: 10.3998/mpub.9970368

ISBN 978-1-60785-452-4 (paper)
ISBN 978-1-60785-453-1 (e-book)

An imprint of Michigan Publishing, Maize Books serves the publishing needs of the University of Michigan community by making high-quality scholarship widely available in print and online. It represents a new model for authors seeking to share their work within and beyond the academy, offering streamlined selection, production, and distribution processes. Maize Books is intended as a complement to more formal modes of publication in a wide range of disciplinary areas.

http://www.maizebooks.org

Contents

Introduction..i

PART I WEBINARS..7

A. "But it's a number, so it has to be true!": An introduction to data literacy, Part I..............9
   Presented by Lynette Hoelter

B. "But it's a number, so it has to be true!": An introduction to data literacy, Part II...........13
   Presented by Lynette Hoelter

C. Where the rubber meets the road: Data literacy in the content areas..............................17
   Presented by Jennifer Colby

D. Information literacy includes data literacy!..20
   Presented by Jole Seroff

E. Close reading: Unpacking the impact language has on how we understand statistics.....24
   Presented by Tasha Bergson-Michelson

F. Real world data fluency: How to use raw data..27
   Presented by Wendy Steadman Stephens

G. Gathering data via action research: A plan for librarians, classroom
   teachers, and students..30
   Presented by Susan G. Ballard

H. Data literacy and voting..34
   Presented by Martha Stuit

I. Making sense of data visualization...38
   Presented by Justin Joque

J. DataBasic.io: Tools & activities that help introduce newcomers to data storytelling.......41
   Presented by Catherine D'Ignazio and Samantha Viotty

K. Data presentation: Showcasing your data with charts and graphs................................44
   Presented by Tierney Steelberg

L. Using Social Explorer to help students gain insight..47
   Presented by Justin Joque

M. Infographics: An instructional lens...50
   Presented by Debbie Abilock, Susan Smith, and Connie Williams

N. Tools for preserving your personal and intellectual privacy.......................................55
   Presented by Wendy Steadman Stephens

O. Big Data and you: Normalizing the practices of privacy..58
   Presented by Jole Seroff

P. The right to obscurity vs. the digital Eye of Sauron..62
   Presented by Susan G. Ballard

Q. Student data privacy: Protecting the personal information
   that informs instruction..65
   Presented by Jennifer Colby

R. DataRefuge: Preserving data and growing literacy...69
   Presented by Justin Schell

S. Science in the wild: How to make the most of citizen science
   projects at your school..72
   Presented by Debbie Abilock, Susan Smith, and Connie Williams

PART II CASE STUDIES 77

PERSONAL DATA MANAGEMENT
1. Your presence on social media 80
   Reviewed by Jennifer Colby
2. Tracking student physical activity in school 83
   Reviewed by Tyler Hoff
3. Amazon Echo Look 86
   Reviewed by Tasha Bergson-Michelson and Kristin Fontichiaro
4. Smart home devices in court 89
   Reviewed by Tyler Hoff
5. DNA mapping 92
   Reviewed by Tasha Bergson-Michelson
6. When insurance gives you a fitness tracker 95
   Reviewed by Wendy Steadman Stephens
7. Hiding from digital marketing 98
   Reviewed by Wendy Steadman Stephens
8. ISP consumer data collection 101
   Reviewed by Tyler Hoff
9. Encrypted data, privacy, and government access 104
   Reviewed by Jole Seroff
10. Protecting your rights through civic engagement 108
    Reviewed by Tasha Bergson-Michelson
11. What is a reasonable expectation of privacy? 111
    Reviewed by Jole Seroff
12. Intergenerational differences and data privacy: Generational shift
    or developmental stage? 116
    Reviewed by Susan Smith
13. Comparing United States and European Union approaches to privacy 120
    Reviewed by Jole Seroff
14. Be strategic! Reading and understanding terms of service and privacy policies 124
    Reviewed by Tasha Bergson-Michelson
15. What does Cambridge Analytica have about you? 127
    Reviewed by Wendy Steadman Stephens

CITIZEN SCIENCE
1. Scientists and citizen scientists: Cooperation and reservations 132
   Reviewed by Kelly Hovinga
2. Candy Crush and Zooniverse: The psychology of citizen science 135
   Reviewed by Kelly Hovinga
3. Citizen science techniques to uncover insights in the humanities 139
   Reviewed by Connie Williams
4. Tour of the Leafsnap leaf identification app 142
   Reviewed by Wendy Steadman Stephens
5. Habitat Network: Learning about and managing the landscape we share ... 145
   Reviewed by Susan D. Ballard

6. Smithsonian Institution Transcription Center 148
   Reviewed by Tyler Hoff
7. Where does federal data go? 151
   Reviewed by Connie Williams
8. Native knowledge meets scientific knowledge through citizen science 155
   Reviewed by Connie Williams
Bonus feature: Choosing a citizen science project for your classroom 159
   Reviewed by Susan Smith, with Connie Williams, and Debbie Abilock

BIG DATA
1. Unroll.me email tracking and data sale 172
   Reviewed by Tyler Hoff
2. Big Data and discrimination 176
   Reviewed by Jo Angela Oehrli
3. Television sets collecting data without notifying consumers 180
   Reviewed by Jole Seroff
4. Big Data and self-driving trucks 184
   Reviewed by Debbie Abilock
5. Predictive policing: The seduction of technology 188
   Reviewed by Susan Smith
6. Big Data in banking and loans 192
   Reviewed by Kelly Hovinga
7. Bias in student predictive analytics data: Does it help or hinder potential
   prospects/relationships? 195
   Reviewed by Susan D. Ballard
8. Cross conversion tracking: Linking in-store purchases with online ads 199
   Reviewed by Kelly Hovinga
9. The ethics of Mechanical Turk 204
   Reviewed by Wendy Steadman Stephens
10. The dark side of data: Using data as a means of stalking, surveilling, or
    preying on vulnerable populations 208
    Reviewed by Susan D. Ballard

ETHICAL DATA USE
1. The personal information you are giving away 214
   Reviewed by Jennifer Colby
2. Protecting student data in schools 217
   Reviewed by Jennifer Colby
3. SAT and ACT information: What happens to it? 220
   Reviewed by Jennifer Colby
4. Surveillance cameras in schools and the case of special education 223
   Reviewed by Susan Smith
5. Student privacy in the age of cloud storage 227
   Reviewed by Susan Smith
6. Big Data and government nudges 230
   Reviewed by Debbie Abilock

7. The fear factor: Hyped-up use of data to sway public opinion/behavior 234
   Reviewed by Susan D. Ballard
8. Those smart devices are smarter than you think 237
   Reviewed by Jennifer Colby
9. Canaries in the mine: Chicago and Flint — haves vs. have-nots in use of data 240
   Reviewed by Susan D. Ballard
10. The implications of privacy regulation on Internet privacy.. 243
   Reviewed by Tyler Hoff
11. Data philanthropy...247
   Reviewed by Tasha Bergson-Michelson

Appendix A: Data literacy rules of thumb..251
Data literacy related standards..259
Creating Data Literate Students..261
Contributors..263
Index..271

Introduction

Every day, your students are immersed in data, whether they're reading their textbooks, viewing infographics in their social media feed, or making sense of the day's news with their families. Data — millions of little "bits" of numbers and information — may be collected, aggregated, and analyzed to determine which coupons their family receives when they show their customer card at the grocery store, whether their family qualifies for a mortgage, the level of energy efficiency in their home, or even what election ads they see on Facebook.

Knowing how to recognize the role data plays in their lives is critical to navigating today's complex world. Yet few high school students are exposed regularly to the kinds of practice with statistics, visualizations, and real-world issues — particularly in the digital age. Graphs in math class, where the y-axis always starts at zero, don't always function the same way in news stories, where the y-axis may be truncated to fit in limited space. If students don't know to "stop, look, and listen" when they confront even the simplest visualizations, their prior experience may contribute to misunderstanding. We assume that today's students can move fluidly between online sites and portals, but they may not realize that their Facebook posts are being scanned by algorithms to determine what they see in their feed. The ease with which our thermostats, exercise trackers, and Instagram accounts collect information about us belies the reality that they may be used to construct hidden profiles about who we are, what we value, and where we shop. Daily, we leave behind bread crumb trails that can be used to adjust the pricing of our merchandise, airline tickets, and more.

Data literacy — the ability to "read" and "write" effectively with data — is critical to success in the 21st century. We want our high school students to graduate being able to understand and make conscious choices about the ways in which they approach data. We recognize that data is not constrained to any particular subject area: in fact, it pervades all subject areas. Additionally, the high school day is tightly regimented, with little room to add coursework in data literacy. We saw a need for nimble just-in-time interventions, mini-lessons, and other strategies that librarians and their classroom colleagues could insert into existing curriculum.

With that in mind, we launched the project Supporting Librarians in Adding Data Literacy Skills to Information Literacy Instruction. Made possible in part by the Institute of Museum and Library Services RE-00-15-0113-15, our goal was to develop the capacity of high school librarians and others to gain skills that they could deploy as-needed across curriculum areas and beyond the classroom and into the wild.

Beginning in 2015, we convened conversations between those who were already fluent in data skills and highly-skilled curriculum leaders to work on three projects:

» **The 4T Virtual Conference on Data Literacy** (http://dataliteracy.si.umich.edu/conference), was a pair of free online conferences for high school librarians and educators (and, as we discovered, over 80 other types of professionals!). In 2016 and 2017, topics included data and voting, basic statistics strategies, sources of raw data, infographics creation, citizen science as a pro-social use of Big Data, personal data management, and more.

» **Creating Data Literate Students** (a free book at http://datalit.sites.uofmhosting.net/books/book/ or available for purchase at cost at https://www.amazon.com/Creating-Literate-Students-Kristin-Fontichiaro/dp/1607854244), our 2017 publication in which our experts unpacked their experiences navigating data with high schoolers. Chapters ranged from a discussion of the most valuable statistical strategies to teach to how to create engaging infographic units to how to find data and conduct basic analysis with Microsoft Excel.

» **This book**, in which we focus on building the professional learning of high school librarians and educators.

The book you are reading now is divided into two sections.

In Part I, you'll be able to access the archived sessions from the 2016 and 2017 4T Virtual Conference on Data Literacy. We've designed these to be "out of the box" professional learning experiences for you and your colleagues and hope you will view these with colleagues in a variety of settings, including professional learning communities, inservice events, and in other small groups. These webinars follow our project's seven themes:

» **Data and statistical comprehension** - Our experts have sifted through statistical practices and identified the most impactful things we need to know about understanding numbers so that we can share that information with our students.

» **Data in arguments** - From the op-ed page to Congressional hearings to essays in English class, data is used to support arguments and thesis statements. How can we help students read more critically and use data to bolster their own arguments effectively?

» **Data visualizations** - Arguably the most popular theme in our project, data visualization ranges from creating simple pie charts to developing complex infographics. The critical questions here are how we "read" and "write" with data in visual form.

» **Big Data** - "Big Data" is an umbrella term referring to the process of collecting large amounts of numerical or informational data and then using algorithms (computer processes) to draw conclusions. Often perceived as infallible, educators and their students need to be aware that algorithms may be purposefully or accidentally skewed and have intended or unintentional consequences.

» **Citizen science** - In the digital era, scientists can now generate and collect incredible amounts of data. Whether that data manifests as weather data, photos of animals, or lab documents, the volume is too great for any one person to analyze. Online portals make it possible for high schoolers to contribute to prosocial projects that embrace the best of the Big Data era ... but what should we be aware of?

» **Personal data management** - From a young age, individuals begin generating data. From social media clicks to browser information, from activity trackers to digital assistants, what should we know so we can help high schoolers be aware of what they should be aware of and can make conscious choices about the degree to which they want to share their data with others?

After viewing each webinar, you'll find discussion questions and activities that you can use to bridge webinar content with your own classroom experiences. (You can also find links to the videos and accompanying materials at http://datalit.sites.uofmhosting.net/books/data-literacy-in-the-real-world/webinar-discussion-sheets/ .)

In Part II, you'll find over 45 case studies related to data "in the wild." These aren't hypotheticals — they're pulled from the news. We invite you and your colleagues to read the resources provided (hint: you can find a list of each case study's links at http://datalit.sites.uofmhosting.net/books/case-study-links/) and engage with the discussion questions. We've taken care to avoid being didactic here: you won't find us saying that certain tools or practices are good or bad — those are decisions each individual should make for him or herself.

We've organized these case studies into four themes:

- » Personal data management
- » Citizen science
- » Big Data
- » Ethical data use

Once you have tried these in professional learning settings, you may wish to bring some of them into your classroom.

Throughout the text, you may encounter long URLs separated with a hyphen at the end of a line. In that case, don't type or include a hyphen when visiting those web pages.

Our work with educators and librarians over the past two years has solidified our belief that these are ideas and concepts worth grappling with, first as professionals and secondly with our students, and we are eager to hear how you are using your new-found knowledge with your students. We encourage you to drop us a line at contact.data.literacy@umich.edu with your insights.

PART I
WEBINARS

A. "But it's a number, so it has to be true!": An introduction to data literacy, Part I

Presented by Lynette Hoelter

This webinar is the first of two that cover the basic concepts of data and data literacy. Data literacy is about asking questions as one encounters numerical information in popular and scientific media. Numbers can be as fallible as any other source of information. This first in a two-part presentation will provide a concrete definition of data literacy, provide examples of the kinds of questions to raise when confronted with data, and give sources of information and types of assignments especially well-suited to building data literacy skills. This first part of the presentation will address the following concepts:

- » Variables
- » Averages (central tendencies)
- » Percentages, percentiles, and percent change

Attendees will acquire the tools needed to begin similar conversations with students. Because working with numerical evidence is, as much or more, a mindset as it is a set of mathematical skills, the content will be helpful for teachers in all disciplines, not just math or science.

Link to video: https://goo.gl/ZjEVSq

Time: Assume this activity will take 90 minutes, (36 minutes for the webinar itself and 54 minutes for a selection of activities and/or discussion questions).

Timeline:
Quantitative literacy: 2:50
Key statistical concepts: 9:10
Variables: 9:40
Percentages: 14:50
Rates: 18:20
Percent change: 20:20
Averages: 22:35
Averages activity: 25:30
Statistic terms in the classroom: 28:20
Recap: 34:48

Related webinar resources:
Google Doc: https://goo.gl/8sFbN5
Slide deck: https://goo.gl/ywPMyt

Discussion questions

1. What jumped out at you as knowledge already familiar to your students from existing curriculum practices?

2. What stood out as a data skills gap that needs to be addressed?

3. Should the skills you have identified be worked into someone's existing curriculum, or should they be taught in a mini-lesson only if they should happen to arise in the classroom?

4. What problems can you or your students solve with the information in the webinar?

5. How can you highlight the differences between statistical literacy and math class for students?

6. What are some ways to show how data collection affects datasets?

7. How can you incorporate statistical literacy gracefully into a class?

8. What are some specific issues or concerns that could arise if you bring statistical literacy strategies into your classroom?

9. When might it be more advantageous to use a percent or a rate instead of a raw number when describing something?

10. How can you explain to students when they should look to use mean, median, or mode?

Recommended activities

1. **Create a data literacy strategy of the week.** Imagine that you could set aside five minutes a week — in your class, in the slideshow that plays in your school hallways, during a school broadcast, and/or in a family newsletter — to share a weekly data literacy strategy with the school. What would you pull out from this webinar to fill that weekly slot?

2. **Brainstorm mean, median, and mode.** Set a timer for five minutes. As individuals, brainstorm as many situations in which calculating the *mean* might be the best type of "average" to compute. Repeat with *median* and *mode*. Then pool

your responses into a common document to share with other educators.

3. **Explain percentile versus percentage to school parents.**
   Create a newsletter blurb for parents and guardians explaining the difference between percentage and percentile that could be slipped into the report card envelope.

B. "But it's a number, so it has to be true!": An introduction to data literacy, Part II

Presented by Lynette Hoelter

This second of two sessions dives further into data literacy concepts, touching on the nature of data, how you can incorporate statistical literacy into the classroom, and how variables play into data analysis and collection. Data literacy is all about asking questions as one encounters numerical information in popular and scientific media. Numbers can be as fallible as any other source of information. This second in a two-part presentation will provide a concrete definition of data literacy, provide examples of the kinds of questions to raise when confronted with data, and give sources of information and types of assignments especially well-suited to building data literacy skills. This second part of the presentation will address the following concepts more closely:

» Sampling
» Margin of error/confidence
» Correlation
» "Controlling" for ...
» Significance

Attendees will acquire the tools needed to begin similar conversations with students. Because working with numerical evidence is as much or more a mindset as it is a set of mathematical skills, the content should be helpful for teachers in all disciplines, not just math or science.

Link to video: https://goo.gl/ZjEVSq

Time: Assume this activity will take 90 minutes, (43 minutes for the webinar itself and 47 minutes for a selection of activities and/or discussion questions).

Timeline:
Recap of Part I: 1:10
Key statistical concepts: 3:05
Sampling and methodology: 3:48
Margin of error: 13:20
Correlation: 17:45
Negative correlation activity: 27:10
Statistical significance: 30:44
In practice/Where to find examples: 35:09
Recap: 40:35

Related webinar resources:
Google Doc: https://goo.gl/H5w3UO
Slide deck: https://goo.gl/6CfjKm

Discussion questions

1. What jumped out at you as knowledge already familiar to your students from existing curriculum practices?

2. What stood out as a data skills gap that needs to be addressed?

3. Should the skills you have identified be worked into someone's existing curriculum, or should they be taught in a mini-lesson only if they should happen to arise in the classroom?

4. What problems can you or your students solve with the information in the webinar?

5. How can you emphasize the different aspects of good sample selection to students?

6. What are some ways you can demonstrate how question wording affects the answers on surveys?

7. Correlation versus causation is a key statistical concept. What are some ways to emphasize the difference between the two using activities the students conduct? What are some resources not in the slides that can be used to emphasize the difference between the two?

8. How can you incorporate statistical literacy gracefully into a class?

9. What are some specific issues or concerns that could arise if you bring statistical literacy strategies into your classroom?

10. How can you teach statistical language to students? What are some ways to emphasize that certain words have different meanings than students might be used to?

Recommended activities

1. **Add to your list of weekly data literacy strategies.** Think back to the weekly data literacy strategy list you made in Hoelter's first webinar (Part I). What could you now add to your calendar of weekly data skills that you could promote

in your class, in the slideshow that plays in your school hallways, during a school broadcast, and/or in a family newsletter? Swap ideas with others in the room so everyone leaves with a robust list.

2. **Practice causation vs. correlation.** Fold a paper in half and set a timer for five minutes. Individually, brainstorm lists of known *causative* relationships (e.g., smoking *causes* cancer). On the right hand side, brainstorm lists of *correlative* relationships (e.g., eating breakfast relates to higher test scores). Then discuss as a group to check your thinking.

3. **Think about sample size in the real world.** Think about the longtime Trident gum commercial tagline: "Four out of five dentists recommend Trident to their patients who chew gum." What is really being said here? What sample size would make you feel more confident about this statement? Can you think of any other commercials or brands that use sample sizes to promote customer confidence?

C. Where the rubber meets the road: Data literacy in the content areas

Presented by Jennifer Colby

Data literacy is useful in all content areas, not just in math class. Having data literate students means you can use data visualizations and raw data to present material in different forms for different learners. Teaching students data literacy also helps prepare them for standardized testing and helps them understand other forms of literacy.

Link to video: https://goo.gl/ZjEVSq

Time: Assume this activity will take 90 minutes (38 minutes for the webinar itself and 50 minutes for a selection of activities and/or discussion questions).

Timeline:
Integrating data literacy: 2:10
Data comprehension: 3:00
Data visualization: 5:15
Data as argument: 5:40
Reasons for data literacy: 7:33
GAP: 20:30
Integration activities: 26:30
Sources for data visualization: 30:15
Developing informed citizens: 31:15

Related webinar resources:
Google Doc with link to slide deck: https://goo.gl/e9scXW

Discussion questions

1. How can standards be addressed with schoolwide data literacy practice?

2. How do standardized test questions change your understanding of the need for cross-curricular data literacy skills?

3. What experiences can you share from your teaching related to student interactions with data and visualizations?

4. What are some ways to collect data in a non-science classroom?

5. How can you use data to present material in a new light?

6. What are some challenges you foresee from using data in this way?

7. What are good sources of data and data visualizations for classroom use?

8. Are there lessons for which you would not want to use data? Why?

9. Is there such a thing as using data-oriented lessons too much? Why or why not?

10. What would you need to adjust in your teaching to make room for discussions about data?

11. Do you see information here that would be helpful for colleagues in other subject areas? Which information? Why?

Recommended activities

1. **Browse the data visualization lesson tips** in the slide deck at http://datalit.sites.uofmhosting.net/2017/03/17/data-literacy-at-macul/ . Think about how these activities would be useful (or could be adapted to become useful) in your classroom. Share out with your group.

2. **Do a search online for infographics** related to your subject area. Check the creator and sources used for credibility. Send links to fellow educators. Brainstorm how you would use them in a lesson.

3. **Browse your state or district learning standards**. Where do they call for data skills? To find related standards, search for terms such as, *visual, quantitative, claim, information*, and *bias*. (Find links to national standards at the back of this book, as well as a link to a list of the data-related standards in those documents.) Make a table. In one column, list the standard's number and text. In the next column, describe how your subject area will work to achieve that standard. Submit the completed document to your administrator, department head, and/or district administrator.

D. Information literacy includes data literacy!

Presented by Jole Seroff

This presentation will provide a big-picture framing for data literacy as a component of information literacy. How do students move through the research process when they begin looking more attentively at how data is "read" and "written"? This webinar dives into the specifics of how you can use data literacy to help students evaluate and use statistics. The session focuses on real-world student activities to develop their ability to benchmark statistics and evaluate the sources of those statistics.

Link to video: https://goo.gl/ZjEVSq

Time: Assume this activity will take approximately 90 minutes (30 minutes to view the webinar, and another hour to do the activities and discussion questions.)

Timeline:
00:00 Introduction of presenter
00:50 Opening thoughts
2:00 Reference to 2007 *Standards for the 21st-Century Learner* (American Association of School Librarians)
3:00 Information literacy definition
3:35 Webinar goals
4:44 Step 1: Explore a new topic
7:01 How to use background reading
8:26 Benchmarking
10:54 Benchmarking activity
17:22 Step 2: Contextualize a statistic
18:41 Step 3: Use data as evidence
21:09 Data as evidence activity
25:47 How to interrogate a statistic

Related webinar resource:
Google Doc #1: https://goo.gl/Awn5Ah

Discussion questions

1. Seroff concentrates on three moments in the information literacy process in this webinar: exploring a new topic ("stepping stone reading"), evaluating an argument, and using data as evidence. Discuss each stage with fellow participants. What do you notice in student behavior at each of these stages? How do they currently respond to data?

2. How do you teach and respond at each stage?

3. How do Seroff's experiences echo your own?

4. What is different from your experience?

5. What resources not mentioned in the webinar can students use to evaluate statistics used in arguments?

6. What exercises can you do with students to help them develop their statistical benchmarking skills?

7. What questions should students be able to ask of statistics while benchmarking them?

8. What role do different media outlets play in teaching students how to benchmark statistics?

9. What do you see students learning from the media about how to use statistics to support their arguments?

10. How can you help students avoid cherry-picking behavior?

Recommended activities

1. **Explore information literacy and the inquiry process.** Seroff references the 2007 *Standards for the 21st-Century Learner*, published by the American Association of School Librarians, available for download at http://ala.org/aasl/standards . Download a copy. Where do you see openings for bringing data literacy into those standards for students?

2. **Learn more about write-arounds from Sara Kelley-Mudie.** Seroff mentions Kelley-Mudie's use of this technique in the first third of her webinar. Visit Kelley-Mudie's blog post "Write arounds for topic selection" (http://kmthelibrarian.blogspot.com/2014/10/write-arounds-for-topic-selection.html) and discuss how this strategy might work with your students.

3. **Brainstorm needed statistical benchmarks.** At 11:00 into the webinar, Seroff modeled finding statistical benchmarks with live participants about video games and violence. Try her process using a topic that your students either study or research in your classroom or library. What kinds of reliable statistical benchmarks would be helpful in helping students contextualize the numerical data they will encounter with this topic? Is it the number of legal voters? The size of the U.S. population? The area of Great Britain and the United States? Then use resources such as http://census.gov, https://www.cia.gov/library/publications/the-world-factbook/, an encyclopedia, or an almanac to identify benchmarks that

you can distribute or post for students to reference. What would a list of benchmarks look like if you added to this list throughout the year?

E. Close reading: Unpacking the impact language has on how we understand statistics

Presented by Tasha Bergson-Michelson

How do the words we use to frame and describe statistics potentially change how readers perceive their meaning? Students often go looking for "some number" to use as evidence, but evocative language in which the statistics are often embedded may go unnoticed, even while it transforms the reader's interpretation of a statistic's meaning. Luckily, applying students' formative skills in literary analysis can go a long way toward helping them move beyond initial responses to successfully analyzing and evaluating data. Come play with the language of statistics — this webinar addresses skills that can be used to assess the use of statistics in text. Bergson-Michelson relates them to the close reading skills many students are already familiar with from English class, before using headlines and an article to demonstrate some of those skills.

Link to video: https://goo.gl/ZjEVSq

Time: Assume this activity will take 90 minutes, (42 minutes for the webinar itself and 48 minutes for a selection of activities and/or discussion questions).

Timeline:
Language activity: 5:00
Structure of statistical storytelling: 7:16
Pure statistical storytelling: 11:00
Correlation vs. causation: 11:54
Causation and correlation activity: 13:20
Language indicators: 25:00
Questions: 26:47

Emotionally evocative statistical storytelling: 30:05
Close reading exercise: 33:05
Recap: 40:41

Related webinar resources:
Google Doc: https://goo.gl/AMzbzB

Discussion questions

1. What are your key takeaways from the webinar?

2. What do you make of Bergson-Michelson's observations of how students approach numbers?

3. What rang particularly true given the students you work with?

4. What lessons can educators learn from English and literature teachers to apply to statistical reading?

5. How can you improve students' statistical vocabulary?

6. Bergson-Michelson discusses the prevalence of field-specific vocabulary. What signs can students use to identify words that have a meaning different from what they are used to?

7. What can educators do to improve students' knowledge of correlation words and causation words?

8. The webinar has lists of words associated with correlation and causation. What activities can you do with students to help them learn these words in an interesting way (e.g., not memorizing)?

9. Question marks are particularly important for indicating meaning in statistical writing. Sometimes they can be a hedge; other times they indicate a lack of causation. How can you tell the difference?

10. Tone is always difficult to convey in text but is one of the most important components of communication. How can students better learn to recognize tone in text?

Recommended activities

1. **Start a collection of clickbait headlines related to statistics and data literacy.** Start a physical or digital file in which you start collecting headlines that use statistics, causation instead of correlation, or other data tricks to entice the reader to click.

2. **Explore language related to causation and correlation.** Visit http://bit.ly/DataLitCloseReading. In small groups, invite participants to complete the first exercise, identifying which of the listed headlines indicate causation and which indicate correlation. Discuss your results as a larger group. What rules of thumb can you take away from this experience to share with students?

3. **Discern the author's perspective.** Visit http://bit.ly/couldyourfastfoodburger and read over the article. Now look at the graphic on the last page at http://bit.ly/DataLitCloseReading. Discuss the article through addressing these three questions featured on the graphic (and also listed below). Think about how you would call on students to support their answers with evidence.
    » What does the author **say** (topic)?
    » What does the author **think** (opinion)?
    » What does the author want me to **do or say** (call to action)?

F. Real world data fluency: How to use raw data

Presented by Wendy Steadman Stephens

High school students don't often get to work with raw data. The collection or generation of data may seem monolithic and unquestionable. Students are more likely to confront data through headlines crafted to entice reader curiosity and stress novelty. This webinar shares several tools and tips for dealing with raw data. In addition to discussing how to deal with raw datasets, this webinar gives participants many resources that have publicly available datasets which are easy to access for students.

Link to video: https://goo.gl/ZjEVSq

Time: Assume this activity will take 90 minutes, (47 minutes for the webinar itself and 50 minutes for a selection of activities and/or discussion questions).

Timeline:
About data literacy: 6:15
Thinking computationally: 8:36
Finding existing datasets: 21:31
Presenting data responsibly: 39:41
Recap: 46:00

Related webinar resources:
Google Doc: https://goo.gl/FGqtRF
Slide deck: https://goo.gl/45qbk0

Discussion questions

1. What are the key themes of the webinar (e.g., the categories of sites she recommends)?

2. What advice from the presenter did you find most resonant?

3. Why does the presenter advocate for using existing datasets instead of just letting kids explore online?

4. Which sites have you used before? Which have been valuable?

5. Which sites might be the most valuable for colleagues and classroom teachers you know?

6. Which dataset do you think would be best for introducing students to datasets in general? Why?

7. Which would you not want to start with? Why?

8. What criteria are you using to determine "best" datasets?

9. Which dataset do you find the most interesting?

10. Which do you think students would find the most interesting?

Recommended activities

1. **Explore the sites Steadman Stephens hand-selected.** View the list of tools at http://tinyurl.com/datafluent. Divide participants into groups, with each exploring one source. Have each group prepare a one-minute tour of their chosen site.

2. **Recommend a dataset to a colleague.** Pass out blank stationery to the group. Ask each person to think of someone else in her building who might be able to benefit from either a site or a dataset within a site. Write them a note letting them know about the dataset and why it might be useful.

3. **Add a dataset to your resource page.** Choose at least one dataset to add to your library or class's web page, social media page, and/or resources page. As an extension, consider adding one site a week to your "data of the week" project you started with Lynette Hoelter's two webinars on statistical literacy. How close are you now to having a year's worth of strategies and resources?

G. Gathering data via action research: A plan for librarians, classroom teachers, and students

Presented by Susan D. Ballard

In today's data-driven world, librarians and educators are under increasing pressure to show that their efforts yield measurable results. Action research (AR) is a flexible framework in which educators can design interventions with assessment in mind, implement those changes, measure the impact, and share the results. This practitioner-friendly approach puts you in the driver's seat. You don't need a Ph.D. in statistics to gather data that matters! In this presentation, you'll learn more about the AR cycle and its power to help you measure and communicate what matters. Once you have used it yourself, you'll be able to teach your students to design their own AR!

This webinar provides an overview of how to use research to benefit your professional life and development. It touches on data collection and analysis techniques, and discusses how you can best adapt research practices to different professional roles and scenarios.

Link to video: https://goo.gl/ZjEVSq

Time: Assume this activity will take 90 minutes (38 minutes for the webinar itself and 50 minutes for a selection of activities and/or discussion questions).

Timeline:
What is action research (AR)?: 2:18
AR to foster collaboration and self reliance: 6:14
Advantages to action research: 7:25
Connection to data literacy: 9:25
Getting started: 13:05
Action research proposal: 13:22
Data usage: 22:06
Reporting the data: 31:20
Application with students: 32:50
Summary and recap: 36:50

Discussion questions

1. What appeals to you about action research (AR) as a pathway to gathering data and insights as an educator?

2. What kinds of data are you asked to demonstrate to your administrator, department chair, district coordinator, or other stakeholders? Which kinds might be conducive to AR?

3. What appeals to you about AR as a technique for students? In what kinds of classes or projects might AR be a useful way for students to collect data?

4. What is a topic, issue or area of interest that you could use AR to study and learn about in order to "take action" in your own classroom or library?

5. What rules of thumb can you take away from this webinar?

6. How can you effectively frame an AR question for yourself? For a student? For another stakeholder?

7. What are some ways you can limit qualitative variables while doing AR in a school environment?

8. What are some best practices for presenting your research results to stakeholders?

9. What presentation styles or formats are preferred by your administration, board, and/or trustees?

10. What are some things to avoid while presenting results?

Recommended activities

1. **Review your school's strategic plan.** Each school or district has a long-term plan, often called a strategic plan, in which areas to receive additional or particular focus are outlined. Identify those priorities.

2. **Identify opportunities for research related to your district's needs or those of your classroom or library.** Are there issues that could be studied via AR that could be useful not only for your classroom but in service toward the larger strategic plan? Brainstorm possibilities.

3. **Read and discuss this case study.** Prior to retirement from Londonderry (NH) School District, Susan D. Ballard was on a team to use AR to research the impact and effectiveness of professional development and practice related to interactive

whiteboards. Read the report at http://datalit.sites.uofmhosting.net/2017/05/14/action-research-example/ and discuss how AR illuminated their practice.

H. Data literacy and voting

Presented by Martha Stuit

This webinar discusses the importance of data literacy on many different aspects of the 2016 U.S. presidential campaign, and politics in general. It addresses the difficulties in assessing electorate polls by exploring how they are created and manipulated before diving into some misuses of data visualizations and some statistical issues related to news coverage of candidates and races.

Link to video: https://goo.gl/ZjEVSq

Time: Assume this activity will take two hours (48 minutes to view the webinar, and another hour to do the activities and discussion questions).

Timeline:
Agenda: 0:00-1:31
News media perception: 1:32
2016 presidential election summary: 3:07
Rule of thumb 1: Knowing polls work: 4:39
How polls trip us up: 7:09
Indications of a good poll: 13:20
Poll examples: 15:32
Rule of thumb 2: Apply statistical skills: 26:46
Statistical skills example: 28:37
Rule of thumb 3: Apply data visualization skills: 32:05
Data visualization skills examples: 33:41
Rule of thumb 4: Look at multiple sources: 42:25
Good sources: 43:43

Slide deck: https://goo.gl/weGb3p

Discussion questions

1. Think ahead to the 2018 midterm elections or other upcoming elections in your area. How might framing data literacy as an election issue be useful in your school community?

2. What experiences have you had as an educator that relate to the webinar?

3. How would you address the issue of media bias (perceived and real) with students?

4. Which kind of poll do you think is the most accurate?

5. Which do you think is the most reliable?

6. What bearing does this information have on lessons since major elections happen only every four years.

7. What statistical questions could you ask of polls that are not included in the slides?

8. What is the relevance of polling and poll modeling on students' day-to-day lives?

9. What are some other circumstances where non-geographically aligned maps could help students learn about a complex topic?

Recommended activities

1. **Compare electoral maps.** Ask small groups to find and compare electoral maps from the 2016 Clinton-Trump election to that of Obama-Romney in 2012. Where in the country did the biggest voting shifts happen? What happens if you make comparisons even further back in recent history?

2. **Explore presidential approval ratings over time.** Invite participants to explore Gallup.com, the site of the well-known polling company, and particularly the site dedicated to daily monitoring of presidential job approval ratings for recent presidents:

    » **Donald J. Trump**: http://www.gallup.com/poll/201617/gallup-daily-trump-job-approval.aspx

    » **Barack Obama**: http://www.gallup.com/poll/113980/gallup-daily-obama-job-approval.aspx

    » **George W. Bush**: http://www.gallup.com/poll/111769/gallup-daily-bush-job-approval.aspx (daily approval ratings began midway through his presidency; for a long-term view, see http://www.gallup.com/poll/116500/Presidential-Approval-Ratings-George-Bush.aspx)

    Ask them to choose a president and tinker with various time ranges. Can they manipulate the way the data looks merely by changing the time period sampled? What time period might make their selected president look particularly strong? Particularly weak? What do they make of this ability to change the message of a graph merely by selecting different dates?

3. **Compare polling data.**
   Go to http://www.publicpolicypolling.com/, a site that tracks presidential polling. Choose the most recent poll from the home page. Compare it to the poll conducted immediately following the 2016 Clinton-Trump election. The week President Trump was inaugurated? What patterns do you notice? What can you learn from reading the summary? The methodology? The raw data?

I. Making sense of data visualization

Presented by Justin Joque

Data visualization is first and foremost a sense-making process; it is a means by which we extract meaning from complex datasets. This presentation will explore the ways that data can be transformed into visual representations and how we can make sense of these visualizations. Discussion will include a variety of types of visualizations and when they are most effective. This talk will briefly include information about tools for making data visualizations, but the focus will be on how to read and understand them. The conclusion will discuss ways in which data visualization and data literacy can be taught in the classroom.

Link to video: https://goo.gl/ZjEVSq

Time: Assume this activity will take 90 minutes, (36 minutes for the webinar itself and 54 minutes for a selection of activities and/or discussion questions).

Timeline:
What is data: 3:50
Drawn/non computational data visualization: 6:10
Understanding data visualization: 7:20
US Census data visualizations: 7:50
Breakdown of data visualization options: 15:45
Information density: 21:30
Recognizing patterns: 26:25
Teaching data visualization: 29:08
Making visualizations: 32:00
Recap: 34:45

Related webinar resources:
Slide deck: https://goo.gl/byYVoX

Discussion questions

1. What forms of data visualization were familiar to you? Unfamiliar?

2. Why might we want to have rules of thumb for students on data visualization? Which strategies strike you as most urgent?

3. What experiences have you had as an educator that relate to the webinar?

4. What kinds of data do you think are best suited to visualization?

5. One important point in the presentation is that data is not neutral: the way it is collected affects the datasets. How can you educate students on this point?

6. Aside from color and type of visualization, what other design choices are most important for displaying data? Why?

7. How might color accidentally communicate unintended emotion in data visualizations? For example, in a visualization about gender, what would be the impact if both genders were represented in hues of pink?

8. How do you know how much data in a visualization is too much? Too little?

9. Mapping data to geographic location is not always the best way visualize data. Brainstorm: When would you want to use a map to visualize data, and when would you not want to?

10. Joque concludes by presenting some questions to ask yourself when viewing any visualization. What questions would you add?

Recommended activities

1. **List and prioritize rules of thumb for visualizations.** In small groups, use a piece of chart paper to brainstorm the rules of thumb or helpful hints that Joque presents in his webinar. Now sort them into groups according to high, medium, and low priority for instruction. Which are "must knows" for students?

2. **Start a collection of sample visualizations.** Browse past issues of newspapers or news journals either in print or online. Create an informal scrapbook of more and less effective visualizations. What makes a visualization weaker? Stronger?

3. **Writearound with visualizations.** WTF Visualizations, despite its non-school-friendly title, gathers weird or awkward visualization examples that can lead to great discussions. Visit http://viz.wtf. Browse until you find a handful of visualizations that are particularly awkward. Print them out and place each in the middle of a large piece of chart paper. Place each at a separate table. Divide the participants into small groups and have them rotate between tables adding comments, feedback, and questions to each visualization. (This is known as a "writearound" activity.) Then pull the group together to discuss. Optional extension: Assign one commented visualization to each group and ask them to remake it so it is more accurate or more effective.

J. DataBasic.io: Tools & activities that help introduce newcomers to data storytelling

Presented by Catherine D'Ignazio and Samantha Viotty

There has been a proliferation of tools created to assist novices in gathering, working with, and visualizing data. The problem is that many of these tools prioritize creating flashy pictures without scaffolding a learning process for newcomers to data analysis and storytelling. In this talk, we showcase the motivations behind creating the free, online platform DataBasic.io. We will demo the tools and activities that DataBasic offers as well as discuss the learning goals that they fulfill. We'll kick off the webinar by talking about creative data literacy and the DIY Art project.

Link to video: http://bit.ly/dlitwebinars

Time: Assume this activity will take 90 minutes (46 minutes for the webinar itself and 50 minutes for a selection of activities and/or discussion questions).

Timeline:
Creative data literacy: 2:43
Data mindset: 3:45
Creative data literacy in a library context: 8:38
Beyond Databasic: 11:32
Databasic.io: 18:14
5-minute activity: 20:40
WordCounter: 25:22
Other Databasic tools: 32:11
Sum up for tools: 37:03
Conclusion and questions: 39:58

Discussion questions

1. How do the presenters define "creative data literacy"?

2. What are some datasets that might be conducive to creative data literacy? What are some methods you can use to make these datasets more accessible and meaningful to non-number thinkers?

3. There are many options for entertaining datasets that will interest your students. How can you pull these datasets into meaningful data visualizations that feed into learning and curriculum goals?

4. What types of teaching styles are more conducive to this creative approach to building data literacy skills? How might you market these skills to your education community?

5. Which curriculum areas are conducive to creative data literacy projects?

6. How can you get a community involved in thinking about how to use data creatively? What kinds of community organizations could you involve?

7. How can you tailor creative data literacy activities to meet different learning styles and different working styles?

8. DataBasic is a powerful tool to teach creative data literacy. What are some of the limitations with the website? What can you do as an educator to overcome these limitations?

9. How might you assess students' work when they use the tools at DataBasic?

10. When would you consider exposing students to broader, more powerful tools, such as Excel or even professional tools like R?

Recommended activities

1. **Divide participants up into four groups. Assign a different tool from** http://databasic.io to each. Ask each group to preview a tool and brainstorm possible curriculum connections. After 15-20 minutes, bring the group back together to swap ideas. Appoint a note taker to record everyone's thoughts and email them to the group.

2. **Spend some time looking throug**h https://itsliteracy.org/diy-data-art-activity-guide/. What activities are suited to your age group or learning goals? What are the cost barriers for these projects? Which educators in your community will be interested in various activities?

3. **Host a one-chapter book club**. Go to http://dataliteracy.si.umich.edu/book and read *Creating Data Literate Students'* Chapter 5, "Manipulating Data in Spreadsheets," by Martha Stuit. How could DataBasic serve as an on-ramp to Excel-based data manipulation?

K. Data presentation: Showcasing your data with charts and graphs

Presented by Tierney Steelberg

Learn to use charts and graphs to answer questions about data! Get answers to questions like: What are some rules of thumb for creating impactful charts? When is it best to use one chart type over another? and, which will readers find easier to swallow, a pie chart or a waffle chart? This webinar addresses how you can present data thoughtfully and effectively in chart and graph form. It discusses aspects of data presentation like color choice, graph type selection, general design decisions, and why certain charts are better for certain kinds of data. Discover new types of charts and rediscover old ones while learning how to put them to use most effectively.

Link to video: https://goo.gl/ZjEVSq

Time: Assume this activity will take 100 minutes (40 minutes for the webinar itself and 60 minutes for a selection of activities and/or discussion questions).

Timeline:
Data visualization warm up: 00:55
General rules of thumb: 2:20
Chart and graph types: 11:19
Pie chart: 11:33
Waffle chart: 15:48
Bar chart: 19:03
Dot plot: 22:02
Line chart: 25:45
Histogram: 29:26
Google Public Data Explorer: 33:40

Related webinar resources:
Slide Deck: https://goo.gl/RS40TV

Discussion questions

1. What information jumped out at you as being particularly significant, important, or even urgent to you? To your students?

2. What forms of representing data were new to you? Familiar?

3. How do they relate to the experiences your students already have with charts and graphs?

4. What are some examples of rules of thumb about visualizing data that you can take away from this webinar?

5. What are some advantages to adding complex aesthetics to a visualization? What are some risks?

6. Discuss as a group which types of charts you prefer for different types of data, and why.

7. Are there any chart types you would always avoid? Are there any that you think are almost always effective?

8. Which is your favorite chart type? Why?

9. Which visualization types do you consider essential? Which would you consider optional considering your student population and curriculum needs?

Recommended activities

1. **Convert to another visualization type.** Find a chart or graph in a newspaper, magazine, or journal. Convert it to another visualization type, including labels. How many different kinds of visualization can your group create? Host a gallery walk to see the variety.

2. **Add to your data of the week list.** If you viewed Lynette Hoelter's two webinars, we encouraged you start making a list of "data of the week" strategies and resources that you could share out via newsletters, school broadcasts, posters, in-school slideshows, etc. What from this webinar could you add to that set? How close to a year or semester's worth of data could you get?

3. **Explore available software.** Open Microsoft Excel or Google Sheets software and explore the kinds of data visualization types that are available to you and your students by default. Become familiar with the options. Alternatively, visit Beam (https://beam.venngage.com/) and play with the default data on coffee consumption. How does the same data look different when different chart styles and color palettes are available? What would you want students to know before they began exploring these visualization tools?

L. Using Social Explorer to help students gain insight

Presented by Justin Joque

Helping students gain context for data can be a challenge. But SocialExplorer.com, which has both free and paid features, can unlock insights by mapping data to a U.S. Map. There's nothing to download — the project is browser-based. Because it has many historical datasets from the U.S. Census and similar sources, and a variety of styles for visualizing data, students spend less time tinkering and more time analyzing data. We will cover both how to export tables and create maps using the built-in tools in Social Explorer. We will pay especially close attention to the visualization and mapping options and discuss possible ways to integrate Social Explorer into assignments. Come learn some strategies from U-M's data visualization librarian for how you can use this tool to scaffold students' data explorations and reveal new insights.

Link to video: http://bit.ly/dlitwebinars

Time: Assume this activity will take about 100 minutes (53 minutes for the webinar itself and 50 minutes for a selection of activities and/or discussion questions).

Timeline:
Introduction: 0:34
Census data: 2:42
Thinking about and choosing data: 5:51
Social Explorer: 13:56
Raw data: 16:30
Visualization: 23:10
Questions set I: 40:12
Lesson plans: 46:35
Recap and questions: 48:25

Discussion questions

1. What are the challenges of working with census data? How might technology help with these challenges? Can technology enhance our capability to gather this kind of information? Why or why not?

2. How does using the United States map to represent data change how you interact with data presented about the U.S.?

3. What are some advantages and limitations of only having access to the 2000 census data in the free version of SocialExplorer.com?

4. What would you try to visualize if you had access to more historical data?

5. When would you recommend students use the different visualization styles (for example dots vs. hotspots) of the Social Explorer map?

6. When would you recommend students use different categories of data (for example, gender, income, ethnicity, mean or median, etc.) in Social Explorer?

7. How much guidance would you give students when they use Social Explorer? What are the features that are useful to know versus essential to know?

8. How might a history class, a science class, or an English class benefit from using Social Explorer?

9. Predict and discuss how census data has changed over time.

10. Can maps ever mislead you about data? Read https://www.washingtonpost.com/news/politics/wp/2017/05/13/at-last-an-electoral-map-thats-to-the-proper-scale/ . All of the maps shown are accurate, yet each tells a different story. How does changing the level of detail at which data was collected (e.g., precinct versus state-level) or adjusting the map's size to represent the impact of votes change how you react to the data?

Recommended activities

1. **Some of Social Explorer's mapping capabilities are present in the U.S. Census Bureau's free tools at** https://www.census.gov/censusexplorer/ . Ask participants to explore this site and discuss possible curriculum connections.

2. **There are many additional Census tools online** at http://census.gov. Divide the participants into groups and assign one group to each of these sites to explore and report back to the group.

    » **U.S. and global population estimates:**
        https://www.census.gov/popclock/
    » **My Congressional District:**
        https://www.census.gov/mycd/
    » **American FactFinder:**
        http://factfinder.census.gov

3. **Explore the Census' visualizations available at** https://www.census.gov/library/visualizations.html .

M. Infographics: An instructional lens

Presented by Debbie Abilock, Susan Smith, and Connie Williams

Visuals and data are ubiquitous in teens' lives; they use them to make decisions every day, in and out of school. For us, they are a call to action. The first part of this webinar focuses on how to read and analyze infographics in a critical manner. Discussions include how to forward an effective visual argument, as well as tips and tricks for breaking down the different elements of effective and ineffective infographics. The second half of this webinar on infographics shares strategies for creating infographics as visual arguments, showing the steps students can take to know how much — and which — data will be needed to tell the intended story through an infographic. Students designers can storyframe data and images to create a visual draft of the infographic design that can be finished by hand or translated into a digital design using a computer graphics application. Presenters include an evaluation checklist and suggest strategies and opportunities for how to begin integrating infographics into your teaching.

The presenters stop occasionally to respond to attendees. While the chat window does not appear in the archived version, feel free to pause the video for discussion in lieu of the live chat.

Link to video: https://goo.gl/ZjEVSq

Time: This was a two-part webinar, so please allow extra time. Assume this activity will take three hours (2 hours 5 minutes to view the two-part webinar and another hour to do the activities and discussion questions).

Timeline:
Introduction of presenter: 00:00 - 3:48
Definition of an infographic: 3:49
Goals for teaching infographics: 6:45
Posters vs. infographics: 8:03
Making arguments with infographics: 12:15
Reading infographics: 25:11
Evaluating infographic arguments: 38:47
Visual design in infographics: 41:10
Data stories: Finding context for data: 45:21
Curating data for context: 59:43
How to teach disciplinary writing and thinking: 1:07:50
Start of Part II Reading vs. creating infographics: 1:11:41
Good infographic structures: 1:21:11
Choosing arguments to present with infographics: 1:28:43
Storyframes: 1:33:05
Using infographics for synthesis: 1:42:26

Related webinar resources:
Slides: https://goo.gl/qmhIZV
"Recipe for an Infographic" Article: https://goo.gl/n9cvDd

Discussion questions

Part I: Rationale and framework for teaching infographics

1. Infographics are not part of learning standards or most required curriculum. What interested your group in studying infographics as a pedagogical tool or strategy?

2. How does the webinar differentiate between a poster and an infographic? How does that difference resonate with you as you consider older digital formats like slide decks?

3. How does this use of claims and arguments change your understanding of infographics?

4. How can "reading from the bottom up" help students think more critically about an infographic?

5. How can you teach Tufte's recommendations for graphical excellence to students?

6. The webinar includes an anecdote about counting the unemployment rate. How could population numbers be used in your class?

7. How can you encourage yourself and your students to look beyond cognitive biases?

8. What resources come to mind right now for "in the wild" infographics?

9. How can you teach benchmarking for data? Brainstorm benchmarks for other topics or questions.

10. While teaching benchmarking, how can you effectively teach heuristics?

Part II: Understanding the story behind the design

1. At the very start of Part II, we hear Susan Smith talking about four different charts containing the same data. Why should we be cautious about our students jumping right into chart/graph generators or infographics software?

2. How does Connie Williams define *storyframing*? Are there other projects in which storyframing on paper could be used as a rough draft for the design?

3. Timelines are a visualization structure students are familiar with from elementary school. What questions and strategies might you pull from this familiar form of visualization and bring into your students' work with infographics?

4. What strategies might you use to help students learn to build story elements into their infographics?

5. What kinds of questions might you suggest that students learn to ask themselves when constructing an infographic?

6. What questions should instructors ask themselves before assigning an infographic?

7. How can storyframing help students check their claim or argument?

Recommended activities

1. **Find and analyze flawed infographics**. Set the timer for five to ten minutes and divide your staff into teams. Go on a flawed infographics hunt. Compete in small teams to find the worst infographic. What makes it so bad? Awkward layout? Lack of claim? Confusing colors or design? Poor or missing sources? More poster than argument?

2. **Apply a rubric**. Read Williams and Abilock's "Recipe for an Infographic" (available at https://goo.gl/n9cvDd) and consider the rubric at the end of the article. Use the rubric to evaluate your group's chosen infographic as if it were student work. How does the rubric as an instructional tool for students help you? How effectively does it serve as an evaluation tool? What other questions arise as you deconstruct your flawed infographic. For example, who might want to use it and why, even if it does not meet your standards for excellence? Why might someone use this infographic to bolster their claim, and what might that claim look like? What strategies might the "bad" infographic use to make it more appealing to viewers?

3. **Draft an infographics assignment**. Based on what you now know about structuring an infographics project and distinguishing it from a poster, brainstorm three ideas for an infographics assignments. If you have existing infographics assignments, consider how you might update them based on the strategies from this webinar.

N. Tools for preserving your personal and intellectual privacy

Presented by Wendy Steadman Stephens

Have you ever searched for something out of idle curiosity only to have targeted advertisements follow you around online? How can you combat the ever-increasing number of corporate entities looking to scrape your (and your students) online browsing information? This session will explore a range of tools to preserve your privacy, including Tor, Ghostery, DuckDuckGo, StartPage, and HTTPS Everywhere, with practical and low-effort options for preserving your personal privacy while maintaining the spirit of inquiry.

Link to video: http://bit.ly/dlitwebinars

Time: Assume this activity will take 120 minutes (60 minutes for the webinar itself and 60 minutes for a selection of activities and/or discussion questions).

Timeline:
Introduction: 3:32
Concept of privacy: 5:51
Chat exercise: 18:23
Privacy tools: 21:37
Personal privacy strategies: 33:14
Chat exercise on strategies: 37:39
Recap and questions: 40:24

Discussion questions:

1. What is your general definition of privacy? How does that definition change (or remain unchanged) when you consider the "real world" versus digital world?

2. Do you use social media sites? What advantages do you see for using these sites? How do they impact privacy? Are you mindful of what you post online? Why?

3. What are your experiences with online tracking? Do you think those experiences were advantageous or an invasion of your privacy?

4. What are your own personal needs in regards to digital privacy?

5. What are some of the issues surrounding encrypting email? How might that manifest in your educational environment?

6. What are some strategies you use for protecting your personal information online?

7. What are some methods you could use to find out how a service you use manages security and privacy?

8. Stephens mentions many different tools that can help with digital privacy. Which one, if any, is best suited for your needs? Why?

9. Stephens mentions unroll.me and the controversy surrounding the sale of personal data (see pages 172-175 for a case study on Unroll.me). The company claims that its terms of

service allow the sale of this data. Since users rarely read and/or understand terms of service, do companies have any responsibilities to make invasive practices better-known to consumers? Why or why not?

10. Stephens states that no one is ever really anonymous on the web. Is that true? Why or why not?

Recommended activities

1. **Pick one of the tools that Stephens describes** and determine whether you could implement it regularly in your school.

2. **In small groups, design a digital privacy awareness lesson plan** for your students.

3. **Read or view one of these readings/documentaries** mentioned by Stephens:
    - » Poitras, Laura. 2015. *Citizenfour*. [United States]: RADiUS TWC.
    - » boyd, danah. 2014. *It's Complicated: the Social Lives of Networked Teens*. New Haven: Yale University Press.
    - » Brunton, Finn, and Helen Fay Nissenbaum. 2015. *Obfuscation: a User's Guide for Privacy And Protest*. Cambridge, Massachusetts: MIT Press.
    - » Pariser, Eli. 2011. *The Filter Bubble: What the Internet Is Hiding From You*. New York: Penguin Press.

O. Big Data and you: Normalizing the practices of privacy

Presented by Jole Seroff

You may have heard of Big Data, the process of collecting millions of pieces of data and drawing conclusions from them. From the metadata that is attached to photographs by default to the kinds of information your browser can reveal, we want you and your students to be aware of the kinds of data being quietly collected in the online and digital world so that you can make savvy, informed decisions. Seroff will share tools and resources to help you engage students and inspire active decision-making about digital privacy.

Link to video: http://bit.ly/dlitwebinars

Time: Assume this activity will take 115 minutes (55 minutes for the webinar itself and 60 minutes for a selection of activities and/or discussion questions).

Timeline:
Introduction: 0:52
Make it meaningful: 1:30
Pwned data activity: 7:10
Data vs. metadata: 13:25
Browsers and ISP activity: 15:50
Privacy and security: 19:10
Apps and permissions: 25:14
Encryption: 33:06
Ethics of personal data privacy: 41:43
Conclusion and questions: 49:20

Discussion questions

1. What are the benefits of being more aware of the data being collected about you? Can you imagine why some people feel they'd rather not know these details?

2. Which kind of password practice (e.g., setting up a password manager, making a list, stringing recognizable words together) feels like the best match for you? Why? How would you rank them in terms of practicality, security, and overall viability in your work and life?

3. Consider the photo metadata section of the webinar. Go through your phone and find your camera and photo settings. Make any adjustments that better fit your needs. Consider why you made the changes you did.

4. Go to the slide showing apps and their encryption in a Venn Diagram. Does anything on that slide change how you feel about the apps you use? Why or why not?

5. Do you see this content having a role in your school's curriculum, family-school engagement, and/or after-school programs? What might that look like? Which ideas are the most important to communicate? What are potential areas of tension, politicking, etc., that you would want to look out for before initiating this activity with minors?

6. During the webinar, Seroff mentioned two tools that make you aware of what kind of browser behaviors can be tracked. You experimented during the webinar with http://clickclickclick.click. Now visit the second site — http://webkay.robinlinus.com — and scroll down to see what the site

claims to know about you. How does this reinforce or shift your thinking? How, if at all, does the information change if you use a different browser? What might the impact be if you used a VPN (virtual private network) such as the one built into the Opera browser?

7. Some phone apps only function when given full access to the user's personal information. Thus, when users try to change their privacy settings the app no longer works. How do you feel about the all or nothing nature of these apps? Why do you think companies have this practice? What factors do you consider to determine whether the service offered by the app is worth the breach in privacy? Where is the tipping point — the moment where you would be willing to purchase the app in lieu of sharing your information?

8. Where would you start a discussion with your students about balancing the ethics of consumer protection with the values of a free market?

9. What do you know about the history of protecting individuals' privacy? How do those historical standards apply in the digital world?

10. A tool like ProtonMail uses extra encryption to protect your messages. What would incentivize you to switch over to an account there? What downsides might you envision? What are the potential downsides of continuing to use unencrypted email?

Recommended activities

1. **Download a browser extension like Ghostery** (https://www.ghostery.com/products/) that is designed to inform you about the tools tracking your browser history. Ghostery works with browsers including Firefox, Chrome, Safari, and Internet Explorer. Now go to five of your favorite websites. How many trackers are on those sites? Which, in Ghostery's pull-down menu, do you decide to keep? Which do you block? How did you decide? Discuss as a group.

2. **Spend ten minutes updating your online passwords, creating an account with a password manager service** (like LastPass, 1Password, or KeePass), and/or setting up two-factor authentication. Make a recurring reminder in your calendar to do this again every three to six months.

3. **Take a stand on one of the privacy decisions discussed in this webinar**. Then:
    - » Create an elevator pitch (a short, 15- to 30-second talk) in which you argue for a position on that issue or advocate for a course of action.

    - » Create a public service announcement (live, podcast, or video) encouraging people to adopt a privacy behavior you endorse.

    - » Create a slide for a school's display screens about the privacy behavior you endorse.

    - » Create a tutorial for how your peers can take action for the privacy behavior you endorse (e.g., walk them through how to change an Android's photo settings).

P. The right to obscurity vs. the digital Eye of Sauron

Presented by Susan D. Ballard

In Tolkien's *Lord of the Rings*, the Eye of Sauron was able to surveille the unsuspecting inhabitants of Middle Earth and using the information he gathered, subject them to his will. As we learned, it was left to Hobbits — rather shy, retiring sorts — to finally set things right and thwart his evil intentions! This session will focus on how the use of data has made it almost impossible for the average person to maintain a low profile in a high tech world. While we value the ability to connect with friends and colleagues via social media and use eCommerce with increasing regularity, do we want those interactions and transactions monitored, collected and used to scrutinize and manipulate our lives? Conversely, has the ability for us to also easily access data and information about others turned us into opportunists who "hack" into other people's personal spaces, or even worse, do we exhibit voyeuristic tendencies and a lack of empathy for others by secretly invading their privacy. What would a hobbit do? We'll discuss strategies to guard your right to obscurity and be more understanding of the need to appreciate this right for others, too.

Link to video: http://bit.ly/dlitwebinars

Time: Assume this activity will take 90 minutes (46 minutes for the webinar itself and 50 minutes for a selection of activities and/or discussion questions).

Timeline:
Introduction: 2:45
Privacy vs. obscurity: 4:29
Obscurity vs. security: 11:09

Security vs. surveillance: 18:22
"The Right to Be Forgotten": 24:24
Conclusion and questions: 30:35

Discussion questions

1. What is the difference between privacy and obscurity? What are the advantages and disadvantages of each?

2. What are some of the benefits to having your data online?

3. Since the early 1900s, companies have been using personal information about individuals to target them for advertising. How are the practices in the current day different and similar?

4. Do you own any loyalty cards? How do you decide whether to sign up for a loyalty card? What has been the advantage of using those cards? How do you balance that advantage with sharing personal information about your consumer habits?

5. Where do you as an individual draw a line with privacy? Consider how necessary Facebook or Linkedin can be to participate in a modern society. For example, school reunions and neighborhood associations often communicate through Facebook. How can a line be drawn to factor in the advantages some people see in social media use?

6. What information do you think is acceptable to have online and openly available? What information should be private? How would legislators successfully create a distinction?

7. Have you or someone you know ever had your personal information compromised? Describe the experience, the result, and how you addressed the situation.

8. How broad should the Right to be Forgotten be? See https://www.ifla.org/publications/node/10320 for more information about the Right to be Forgotten.

9. What does the Right to be Forgotten mean for those who have passed on? What does it mean for their loved ones?

10. How do the issues of digital privacy fit (or not fit) into your school's culture, practices, and curriculum?

Recommended activities

1. **Explore the kinds of consumer information available, in part, by merging consumer and other data.** Visit ESRI Tapestry at http://www.esri.com/landing-pages/tapestry and type in your zip code. How does the information resonate with what you know about your area? Are there errors or overgeneralizations?

2. **Consider the kinds of mail you receive each week.** Ask yourself how you may have ended up on that mailing list: from credit reports or other consumer data? From shared catalog lists? Visit the website of the Federal Trade Commission (FTC) at https://www.consumer.ftc.gov/articles/0262-stopping-unsolicited-mail-phone-calls-and-email and read about how you can minimize unsolicited contacts.

3. **Schedule a time to check your credit report**, which you can do annually at no cost and with no impact on your credit score. Visit https://www.usa.gov/credit-reports to learn more.

Q. Student data privacy: Protecting the personal information that informs instruction

Presented by Jennifer Colby

Using student data to develop and inform school curricula and classroom instruction is useful and effective, but we need to weigh the benefits of using this data for school improvement with the dangers of exposing students' personal information. If we understand student data privacy we can be better stewards of our students' personal information.

Link to video: http://bit.ly/dlitwebinars

Time: Assume this activity will take 100 minutes (50 minutes for the webinar itself and 50 minutes for a selection of activities and/or discussion questions).

Timeline:
Introduction: 0:41
Student data: 1:08
Types of student data: 3:45
What is done with student data: 10:20
Threats to student data: 15:27
How to protect student data: 20:46
National level: 21:04
State level: 25:06
Local level: 27:20
Personal plan of action: 31:20
Conclusion and questions: 38:04

Discussion questions

1. What kinds of student data do you collect? Where do you store it? Where do school officials and/or district store it?

2. How long is student data retained in your school district? Why do you think the data is retained for that time period? If you do not know how long student data is retained, how would you find out? What do you think is a reasonable amount of time to save student data?

3. Many teachers and librarians use apps and web-based software that have not been through a district-wide vetting process such as blogging software and web-based educational games. Do you sign your students up for third-party accounts or require that they do? What kind of information is collected about your students by those companies?

4. What do you do to protect your students' data?

5. Consider the information about state laws and student privacy found in the Center for Democracy & Technology's State Student Privacy Law Compendium (https://cdt.org/files/2016/10/CDT-Stu-Priv-Compendium-FNL.pdf). Look up the state laws for your state and consider how you would communicate those laws to your students, parents, administrators, and community. Several states do not have student privacy laws. If you live in one of those states, how might you use other state laws to influence your state legislature?

6. Do we need to collect as much student data as we do? Why or why not? What kinds of data should be time-limited and purged on a regular, scheduled basis? What kinds should be maintained? How did you come up with your decisions?

7. Are students aware of the data you collect about them? Why or why not? How might students become more aware of this data?

8. Consider your own social media accounts. If you were a student, how would college admissions offices view your online social behavior? How would the parents of your students? Your administrators?

9. What kind of student data is stored on your own devices? How is it protected?

10. Could you do a data dump to remove student data from your devices? What would you do to perform a data dump? What can you do to encourage others to protect and remove student data from their own devices?

Recommended activities

1. **Create a graphic** describing how specific student data "travels" through your own school district.

2. **Pick one of the items on the slide labeled "Plan of Action: What Can You Do Now?"** Choose one of the action plans and apply it to your class/school/school district.

3. **The Electronic Frontier Foundation** published a 2017 report on student data and privacy that includes several real-world examples. Download *Spying On Students: School-Issued Devices and Student Privacy* at https://www.eff.org/wp/school-issued-devices-and-student-privacy and choose a few of the page-long case studies for discussion. In small groups, discuss how your school or district would

respond to each situation. When uncertain, circle back to administration for answers. Over the course of a few additional meetings, come up with protocols to address these concerns in your organization.

R. DataRefuge: Preserving data and growing literacy

Presented by Justin Schell

Schell discusses the origins and continued efforts of the DataRefuge movement. Born out of fears of widespread removal of environmental and other governmental data that citizens and corporations alike rely on, DataRefuge has assisted in coordinating more than 40 "Data Rescue" events, bringing together librarians, developers, scientists, archivists, and other concerned citizens to archive a variety of federal data. The project has evolved into a multi-field conversation about the importance, and uneven vulnerability, of data. One of the main lessons of this project is the variety of ways that people can get involved in such preservation efforts. Schell will discuss a number of ways that participants and their students can assist in the project.

Link to video: http://bit.ly/dlitwebinars

Time: Assume this activity will take 100 minutes (50 minutes for the webinar itself and 50 minutes for a selection of activities and/or discussion questions).

Timeline:
What is DataRefuge: 2:52
First iteration: 3:50
Support and pre-existing programs: 6:12
Questions before working: 7:34
Questions I: 11:34
Workflow: 16:46
Results: 25:22
Questions II: 26:09
Current iteration of DataRefuge: 28:04

How you can help: 34:11
Recap and questions: 40:19

Discussion questions

1. How does Schell define data? How would you define or re-define data given the purpose of Data Rescue events?

2. When selecting materials to undergo a Data Rescue project, which criteria are important for selection? Why do you think those criteria are important?

3. What are some of the limitations and benefits to letting data rescue participants choose which websites they focus on?

4. How might surveys to scientists asking them to identify valuable government datasets be a useful method of prioritization? How might it limit archival practices?

5. What are some of the workflow difficulties discovered during early DataRefuge events? How do the workflow parameters influence how people can participate in this type of data rescue?

6. Where should data rescuers draw the line when they have to choose between preserving important versus vulnerable data?

7. Is the data rescue movement more effective as a bottom-up grassroots movement or as a top-down organized movement? Why?

8. If the movement is going to rely on grassroots volunteerism, how can we frame the complexities of data rescue into an activity in which novices can contribute successfully?

9. How might your classroom or school become more aware of the importance of federal data? What can you do at a classroom level to help with this effort within your broader curriculum?

10. Is there data you work with that you think is vulnerable? If so, what steps can you take to make it less vulnerable and/or more accessible? How does student privacy factor into your decision-making?

Recommended activities

1. **Go to the Wayback Machine** (https://archive.org/web/) and type in some common URLs. Explore archived versions of three to five websites. Compare those websites to the current version of those sites. What is different? What is the same? Why do you think it was important for those websites to be archived?

2. **The data rescue movement has focused on preserving data at the federal level. Is there data at your community level that is vulnerable?** How can your school work to preserve it?

3. **Make a plan** for how your school or classroom could participate in rescuing data in some way.

S. Science in the wild: How to make the most of citizen science projects at your school

Presented by Debbie Abilock, Susan Smith, and Connie Williams

Abilock, Smith, and Williams invite you explore the many ways that citizen science projects can fit into your classroom in order to build student skills, collaboration, and confidence. Together we will explore the process of incorporating citizen science projects into a specific course or curricular area. We will review university, governmental, and non-profit portals that offer projects, and the pros and cons of the formats and goals. We will also discuss how to discern an organization's perspective, identify funding and scientific oversight, and how to best match your curricular objectives to a project.

Link to video: http://bit.ly/dlitwebinars

Time: Assume this activity will take 120 minutes (55 minutes for the webinar itself and 60 minutes for a selection of activities and/or discussion questions).

Timeline:
Introduction: 1:30
Hypothetical projects: 5:10
Citizen science definitions: 7:23
Classroom integration: 12:25
Classroom assessment: 16:14
Creating or finding a project: 22:52
Education/curriculum standards: 34:14
Fun vs. engaging projects for your classroom: 36:16
Recap and questions: 42:24

Discussion questions

1. How might citizen science projects contribute to your students' understanding of science? How might humanities teachers use crowdsourcing projects designed for use in citizen science online portals?

2. What elements would need to be in place, and what might students learn, in an ideal citizen science or crowdsourcing project?

3. How might citizen science projects contribute to your students' sense of community or global engagement?

4. What "soft skill," service learning, or socioemotional benefits might accrue from participation in citizen science projects?

5. Discuss how much expertise you think is needed to participate in different types of citizen science projects.

6. What are the advantages and disadvantages of letting students pick their own projects versus committing a class to the same single project?

7. How do you think that screen-based projects differ from "in the field" projects in terms of student engagement and learning?

8. Consider Susan Smith's discussion about how to plan your citizen science project. Are there scientists or other people outside of your school who might want to partner with you? How might you find a local partner and establish a collaborative partnership?

9. What methods might you use to assess citizen science projects in your classroom or school? Why?

10. Citizen science can be deployed during class time, but also consider it as a community outreach activity. Imagine what it would look like to add a citizen science tag-a-thon activity — a time when volunteers come together to label online content — to your school calendar? Would you invite families? Community members? Partners from not-for-profit communities? Combine it with an existing event like parent-teacher conferences or Science Fair or create a standalone? How would you organize it?

Recommended activities

1. **Browse the physical or virtual citizen science projects curated at *Scientific American*** (https://www.scientificamerican.com/citizen-science/). Apply the presenters' method for deciding on a project to your own context. What, if anything, do you think you need from your educational community in order for your class/your school to start or participate in a citizen science project? (Note: If you find a project that interests you, be sure to click through to see if it currently needs volunteer support.)

2. **We often ask our K-12 students to engage in inquiry about the natural world. Zoom over to Zooniverse.org, another digital portal to numerous online citizen science efforts. Take a look at the Michigan ZoomIn project**, a University of Michigan project which features motion-activated photographs of Michigan wildlife. Which animals are familiar to you from your own area? How does that familiarity impact the way you approach the identification work? Now take a look at another wildlife project on the site like

Penguin Watch, Wildwatch Kenya, or Elephant Expedition (all were active at press time). How does your curiosity react differently to these less familiar surroundings and species? What kinds of inquiry-oriented questions arise by engaging in various habitats? How might those kinds of "aha moments" make their way into your classroom?

3. **Take a look at the Smithsonian Institution's transcription project** at http://transcription.si.edu, where several text-based artifacts from the museum's collection await volunteer transcription. How do the currently-available projects resonate with you as potentially useful as an academic or service learning project? Try transcribing an item or two. How much time does each item take? What coding structures did you need to acquire prior to use?

PART II
CASE STUDIES

PERSONAL DATA MANAGEMENT

1. Your presence on social media 80
2. Tracking student physical activity in school 83
3. Amazon Echo Look 86
4. Smart home devices in court 89
5. DNA mapping 92
6. When insurance gives you a fitness tracker 95
7. Hiding from digital marketing 98
8. ISP consumer data collection 101
9. Encrypted data, privacy, and government access 104
10. Protecting your rights through civic engagement 108
11. What is a reasonable expectation of privacy? 111
12. Intergenerational differences and data privacy: Generational shift
    or developmental stage? 116
13. Comparing United States and European Union approaches to privacy 120
14. Be strategic! Reading and understanding terms of service and
    privacy policies 124
15. What does Cambridge Analytica have about you? 127

1. Your presence on social media

Jennifer Colby

Today we connect ourselves and share information on multiple social media platforms. Have you ever thought about who sees this information? Sure your friends and family can see what you have been up to, but what about prospective colleges and employers? Your digital footprints are everywhere and anyone (including colleges) can know just about anything about you. Sometimes we may share too much information — and sometimes we don't know who is collecting it. Our social media accounts project an image about who we are and then people make judgements about us. Sometimes we are not in control of how that information is shared by others. Think about your presence on social media and how it can affect what people think about you.

Resources

DesMarais, Christina. 2013. "11 Simple Ways to Protect Your Privacy." *Time*, July 24. Accessed May 28, 2017. http://techland.time.com/2013/07/24/11-simple-ways-to-protect-your-privacy/ .

Gilpin, Caroline Crosson. 2017. "Will Social Media Help or Hurt Your College and Career Goals?" *New York Times*, Feb. 24. Accessed May 28, 2017. https://www.nytimes.com/2017/02/24/learning/will-social-media-help-or-hurt-your-college-and-career-goals.html . (Note: This article contains links to two separate articles with opposing viewpoints.)

Knorr, Caroline. 2016. "Watch What You Tweet: Social Media Can Affect College Admissions. *CNN*, Sept. 21. Accessed May 28, 2017.

http://www.cnn.com/2016/09/21/health/kids-social-media-college-admissions/ .

Sheninger, Eric. 2017. "Your Digital Footprint Matters." *Huffington Post*, Jan. 8. Accessed May 28, 2017. http://www.huffingtonpost.com/eric-sheninger/your-digital-footprint-ma_b_8930874.html .

Discussion questions

1. What is social media? List different social media platforms.

2. What are the benefits of engaging in social media? What are the drawbacks?

3. Do you have a digital footprint on social media? If so, list the social media platforms that you engage in.

4. What is the difference between and active and passive digital footprints? Can you give examples of each? Do you know who is actively collecting data from you? Do you know who is passively collecting data from you? Make a list for each type of data collection.

5. Consider your digital profile on the various social media platforms you engage in. How would prospective colleges and employers (correctly or incorrectly) make judgments about you based on only the limited information they have from social media? Do you think your digital profile on social media will hurt or help your college and career goals? Why or why not?

6. Do you think it is important to limit your digital footprint? Why or why not?

7. What can you do to "clean-up" your social media profile? Should you?

8. What steps can you take to protect your digital information?

9. What would you have to do to get off the electronic grid in order to not digitally share any information? Is it worth your time and effort? Why or why not? Consider this image – http://imgur.com/gallery/zebhR .

2. Tracking student physical activity in school

Tyler Hoff

Fitness tracking has become a standard part of any American initiative to improve physical fitness. Fitness tracking is now synonymous with wearables like Fitbits and Apple Watches. These devices have the capability to track fitness information, location and other health information. Oral Roberts University opened in 1965 with a rare fitness requirement for incoming students. In January 2016, the school announced it would require incoming freshmen to purchase and use a Fitbit, with a steps per week and average heart rate requirement. This data is stored in a secure database, to which school officials, including professors, have access. This sheet is intended to briefly inform about this issue, present some background resources, and provide sample discussion questions for students.

Resources

Bigelow, William. 2016. "Oral Roberts U Will Require Freshman [sic] to Wear Fitbit Devices." *Breitbart*, January 11. Accessed May 30, 2017. http://www.breitbart.com/big-government/2016/01/11/oral-roberts-u-will-require-freshman-to-wear-fitbit-devices/ .

Chasmar, Jessica. 2016. "Oklahoma University Requires Freshman [sic] to Wear Fitbit, Track 10k Steps Per Day." *Washington Times*, January 11. Accessed May 30, 2017. http://www.washingtontimes.com/news/2016/jan/11/oklahoma-university-requires-freshmen-to-wear-fitb/ .

Machkovech, Sam. 2016. "Evangelical University Requires Fitbit Ownership, Data Syncing for Freshmen [Updated]." *Ars Technica*, February 1. Accessed May 30, 2017. http://arstechnica.com/gadgets/2016/02/evangelical-university-requires-fitbit-ownership-data-syncing-for-freshmen/ .

Root, Jonathon. 2016. "How Fitbit Helps a Conservative Evangelical College Monitor Students' Bodies for Christ." *Religion Dispatches*, March 10. Accessed May 30, 2017. http://religiondispatches.org/where-oral-meets-orwell/ .

Discussion questions

1. Does this case surprise you? Why or why not?

2. Would this requirement be reasonable if it were an elementary school? Middle school? High school? How would you feel if your school had this requirement?

3. Part of Oral Roberts University's mission is to educate the whole student, and students enroll with full knowledge of the fitness and Fitbit requirement. Is the Fitbit requirement reasonable or unreasonable? Before Fitbits, students logged their activity in a journal. Does this change your answer?

4. The University would be able to track student location, as well as fitness information, even while students are off campus or school is not in session. Does this change your opinion? The school has made clear that students are only required to log steps and heart rate information. Does this change your answer? While students are only required to log those two, they would have to opt out of location tracking on the models with that feature. How does this affect your response?

5. Should all professors have access to the data from the Fitbits? Why or why not?

6. It is probably only a matter of time until Oral Roberts' database is hacked. Does this affect your answer?

7. Oral Roberts University was already one of the healthiest universities in the United States before the Fitbit initiative. Given this information, do you think the Fitbit plan is necessary? Why or why not?

3. Amazon Echo Look

Tasha Bergson-Michelson and Kristin Fontichiaro

When you are choosing an outfit to wear do you like getting feedback from other people? Do you wish someone would help you find the kinds of clothes you like faster? And that they fit perfectly? All these benefits are promised by Amazon's Echo Look, a hands-free, voice-activated, Internet-connected device with a camera and two-way speakers. It takes pictures of you wearing different outfits and makes an automated judgement on which is the best. Amazon hopes to use the images users take to better understand the clothing they like, know what looks best on them, and to eventually be able to make clothing fit specifically to an individual, on demand. Consumer advocates worry that the wide range of information recorded by the Look could be harmful to users.

Resources

Campbell-Dollaghan, Kelsey. 2017. "Amazon's New AI Selfies Machine Is The Privacy Parable For Our Time." *Fast Company Design*, April 27. Accessed June 11, 2017. https://www.fastcodesign.com/90112048/amazons-new-ai-selfie-machine-is-the-privacy-parable-for-our-time .

Cooper, Daniel. 2017. "Why Amazon Wants to Replace Your Mirror with a Camera." *Engadget,* April 27. Accessed June 11, 2017. https://www.engadget.com/2017/04/27/what-amazon-gets-out-of-putting-a-camera-in-your-closet/ .

Larson, Selena. 2017. "Amazon's $200 Echo Look Will Judge Your Outfits." *CNN,* April 26. Accessed June 11, 2017. http://money.cnn.com/2017/04/26/technology/amazon-echo-look/ .

Moorhead, Patrick. 2017. "Why Amazon Really Created Echo Look, A Camera In Your Bedroom and Bathroom." *Forbes*, April 27. Accessed June 11, 2017. https://www.forbes.com/sites/patrickmoorhead/2017/04/27/why-amazon-really-created-echo-look-a-camera-in-your-bedroom-and-bathroom/2/#13ca24ca55e5 .

Tufekci, Zeynep. Twitter Post. April 26, 2017, 9:01 am. https://twitter.com/zeynep/status/857263409561317377 . (Note: scroll down to see the entire thread.)

Discussion questions

1. Is this a device you would like to own? Why or why not?

2. What are the advantages of this $200 tool for people? What are the disadvantages? How might this tool help you feel more ready to face the world?

3. According to the promotional photos, for whom is this device intended? Women only? Women and men? Does the target audience change how you feel about the device?

4. What might you give up for this device to work? How might you be rewarded for giving up that data?

5. Whose standards determine whether you look good? You might think of how the system could privilege a certain cultural, ethnic, or stylistic group or even the "look" of particular designers. How will you know what data was used to train the algorithm into passing judgment on your fashion sense? Whose standards would you want judging you?

6. What else gets recorded, as Amazon Look is on all the time? In the promotional photos, Look is placed in the bedroom. Does that make this device different from other automated home devices like the Amazon Echo, Apple HomePod, or Google Home, which are more likely to be placed in a home's more public spaces?

7. What could a company learn about you merely by "seeing" what you are wearing? In other words, what else might the camera be able to "see"?

8. Professor Tufecki's Twitter thread begins by unpacking her concerns about the Amazon Look but then connects those issues to other, broader issues about privacy. To what degree do you agree with her overall line of thinking? Does any part of her thread bring up new reactions or thoughts about privacy or protecting personal data?

9. Some machine learning projects that are being designed to auto-identify the objects in the photo do a better job identifying Caucasian faces as humans than African-American faces. What would the implications be if Amazon Look is better at working with one skin type than another?

10. How might you feel if the system were to tell you your favorite outfit doesn't make the grade?

11. What are the potential benefits/risks of this tool on someone's self-esteem? Does the fact that the marketing materials show the Look being used only by females color your answer?

4. Smart home devices in court

Tyler Hoff

New smart home devices like the Amazon Echo, Apple HomePod, and Google Home work by listening to what you say and transmitting that data to a third party. They are only actively recording and transmitting when a keyword is used. However, they are always passively listening for that keyword. This means there is the possibility of audio recordings of illegal activity not obtained by the police and without the explicit consent of the person being recorded which could be useful for a criminal investigation. This issue was recently brought to a head by a murder case in Arkansas where Amazon refused a warrant for the recordings of the Echo sitting on the suspect's counter. This sheet is intended to briefly inform about this issue, present some background resources, and provide example discussion questions for students.

Resources

Holt, Lester. 2016. "Police Demand 'Amazon Echo' Data as part of Arkansas Murder Investigation." *NBC News*, December, 27. Accessed May 30, 2017. http://www.nbcnews.com/nightly-news/video/cops-demand-amazon-echo-data-as-part-of-arkansas-murder-investigation-842351172001 .

Mele, Christopher. 2016. "Bid for Access to Amazon Echo Audio in Murder Case Raises Privacy Concerns." *New York Times,* December, 28. Accessed May 30, 2017. https://www.nytimes.com/2016/12/28/business/amazon-echo-murder-case-arkansas.html .

Roberts, Jeff. 2016. "Police Ask Amazon's Echo to Help Solve a Murder." *Fortune,* December 27. Accessed May 30, 2017. http://fortune.com/2016/12/27/amazon-echo-murder/ .

Selyukh, Alina. 2016. "As We Leave More Digital Tracks, Amazon Echo Factors in Murder Investigation." *NPR*, December 28. Accessed May 30, 2017. http://www.npr.org/sections/alltechconsidered/2016/12/28/507230487/as-we-leave-more-digital-tracks-amazon-echo-factors-in-murder-investigation .

Discussion questions

1. Does this case surprise you, or were you familiar with it?

2. Echos only begin "listening" when a keyword, also called a wake word, like "Alexa" or "Echo" is used. With this information, do you think there would be anything useful on an Echo in most cases? However, the voice recognition technology is not perfect and there are plenty of stories of Echos activating without the wake word. Does this change your answer?

3. Should people expect to have private conversations around smart home devices like the Echo?

4. Is data recorded and stored by automated devices like Echos different from a voicemail or electronic document created by the same person? Why?

5. Police discovered from another device in the Arkansas home that there was an unusual level of water use around the time of the murder. Should data recorded by smart home devices be covered by the heightened legal expectation of privacy in the home?

6. In 2014, the FBI requested Apple break into a user's iPhone during the investigation of the San Bernardino shooting. How is this case different? The same?

7. Does this case change how you feel about the Echo? How?

8. Sometimes, phones are banned in schools, but smartwatches with voice activation (like Apple Watch's Siri) are increasingly common. Does this kind of technology concern or excite you? Does this change the kinds of things you would say in school (whether you are an educator or a student)? Support your argument with evidence.

5. DNA mapping

Tasha Bergson-Michelson

Over the past several years, the cost of mapping an individual's DNA has dropped dramatically. Now, many companies offer genomic sequencing services for as little as $99. Some consumers participate to find out where their ancestors come from, others to check if they have an increased likelihood of genetic diseases. Scientists argue that massive databases of wholly-sequenced individuals will allow them to compare and figure out what gene combinations indicate complex genetic diseases. They also tout the promise of personalized medicine, matching specific medicines and other cures to an individual's specific genetic makeup. But other scientists argue that the science is not yet precise; privacy advocates worry about the implications of having access to such in-depth genetic data on individuals. What is the best choice for humanity as a whole?

Resources

Data Privacy Lab. 2013. "How Unique Are You?" Harvard University. Accessed June 9, 2017. https://aboutmyinfo.org/index.html .

EuroGentest. 2017. "What Is a Genetic Test?" Center for Human Genetics, January. Accessed June 9, 2017. http://www.eurogentest.org/index.php?id=622 .

National Human Genome Research Institute (NHGRI). 2015. "Privacy in Genomics." National Institute of Health, April 21. Accessed June 9, 2017. https://www.genome.gov/27561246/privacy-in-genomics/ .

Tanner, Adam. 2013. "Harvard Professor Re-Identifies Anonymous Volunteers in DNA Study." *Forbes*, April 25. Accessed June 9, 2017.

https://www.forbes.com/sites/adamtanner/2013/04/25/harvard-professor-re-identifies-anonymous-volunteers-in-dna-study/ .

Winston, Joel. 2017. "Ancestry.com Takes DNA Ownership Rights from Customers and Their Relatives." *ThinkProgress,* May 17. Accessed June 9, 2017. https://thinkprogress.org/ancestry-com-takes-dna-ownership-rights-from-customers-and-their-relatives-dbafeed02b9e .

Zimmer, Carl. 2016. "When DNA Differences Matter." *Scientific American,* Aug. 26. Accessed June 9, 2017. https://www.scientificamerican.com/article/when-dna-differences-matter .

Discussion questions

1. How does the privacy risk of DNA testing weigh against the benefits from having large-scale databases?

2. What do you think are the most compelling risks of donating your DNA for testing? What do you see as the most compelling rewards?

3. Who should be deciding what happens with an individual's DNA: The individual? Scientists? Service providers? The government? What factors did you consider in forming your response?

4. Currently, the cost of genetic testing for health purposes can still be quite high, especially since most people need specially trained medical professionals to help them understand their results. If health insurance companies covered the cost of this testing and follow-up consultations, what would some of the possible implications be for consumers? Would

it affect everyone the same way? If not, what might some of the differences be?

5. What would the impact be if those with insurance were receiving genetic testing and those without insurance were not? What could the possible long-term consequences be? What do you think about those potential consequences?

6. Visit the Harvard site at https://aboutmyinfo.org/index.html. Test how easy or hard it is to identify you from some simple personal facts. What do you think the point of this site is? What do you conclude from having entered the data? How hard would it be to identify you from this data?

6. When insurance gives you a fitness tracker

Wendy Steadman Stephens

Health insurers have begun using activity data collected from wearable devices to provide either cash incentives or deductible rebates to active individuals. With a goal of long-term cost savings through overall health improvement, the attraction for insurers (and the employers that underwrite so many Americans' health coverage) is clear, but overall the use of 24/7 wearable technologies has privacy implications. Wearables have the potential to provide justification for denying coverage to individuals deemed inactive or unhealthy, or increasing insurance rates based on information collected. The *Denver Post* reports that employers are expected to incorporate more than 13 million devices into wellness programs by 2018. Currently, the emphasis is on wearables to increase awareness of the level of activity and health indicators, but is it a slippery slope from incentivizing healthy behavior to requiring it?

Resources

Boyd, Andrew. 2017. "Could Fitbit Data be Used to Deny Health Coverage?." *U.S. News and World Report*, February 17. Accessed May 30, 2017. https://www.usnews.com/news/national-news/articles/2017-02-17/could-fitbit-data-be-used-to-deny-health-insurance-coverage .

Cook, Tracy M. 2016. "Payouts of fitness tracker not just in health benefits — they're monetary, too." *Denver Post*, September 18. Accessed May 30, 2017. http://www.denverpost.com/2016/09/18/fitness-tracker-payouts-health-benefits-money/ .

Japsen, Bruce. 2016. "How Insurance and Wearables Will Change Healthcare." *Motley Fool*, March 13. Accessed May 30, 2017. https://www.fool.com/investing/general/2016/03/13/how-insurers-and-wearables-will-change-healthcare.aspx .

Martin, Alan. 2015. "Step and Save: The Truth About Wearables and Health Insurance." *Wareable*, May 21. Accessed May 30, 2017. https://www.wareable.com/wearable-tech/step-and-save-the-risks-of-using-fitness-tracker-to-save-on-your-insurance-premium-1163 .

Olson, Parmy. 2014. "Wearable Tech is Plugging into Health Insurance." *Forbes*. June 19. Accessed May 30, 2017. https://www.forbes.com/sites/parmyolson/2014/06/19/wearable-tech-health-insurance/#7eff792f18bd .

Discussion questions

1. Do you wear a fitness tracker? If so, what motivated you to purchase it? How closely do you monitor your data and make decisions based on what the tracker tells you?

2. Many corporate health strategies require intermittent monitoring, but insurers concerned with overall wellness have the potential to require round-the-clock wearable use. Do you feel corporations should be able to mandate activity outside the workplace? If you forget to charge your wearable, should you be penalized? What about other personal health decisions: should an employer have the right to ask you to put on a seat belt? Not smoke? Not to drink alcoholic beverages? When and where does an employer have the "right" to control after-hours behaviors? Where would you draw the line in your own life?

3. As the capabilities of wearable health devices improve and increasing quantities of customer data is accumulated, companies will likely gain the potential to diagnose illnesses through improved sensors and big data analysis. How could insurance companies deny coverage or set rates based on preexisting conditions as collected by wearables?

4. Could employees have granular control over the types of information, how long it is stored, and whether it is portable between insurers? Does it matter if you can opt in and out of individual tracking features?

5. Do you think employers should be able to access raw fitness data? Should they be allowed to gamify workplace wellness by comparing employee metrics to recognize and promote healthy behaviors? Why or why not?

6. Some auto insurers encourage drivers to install monitoring devices in their vehicles in exchange for a discount. (For an overview of this, see https://cars.usnews.com/cars-trucks/best-cars-blog/2016/10/how-do-those-car-insurance-tracking-devices-work .) These devices are known formally as telematics-based tracking, and insurance companies often promote them to potential customers by saying that safe driving deserves a reward in the form of insurance discounts. Once installed, telematics devices tap into a vehicle's internal computer to capture data about speed, distance, time spent driving, braking actions, and/or location. Is providing health information different from driving information? How? What kind of security or privacy do you expect your driving data to have?

7. Hiding from digital marketing

Wendy Steadman Stephens

After realizing Internet corporations had intuited her engagement from online interactions, sociologist Janet Vertesi decided to treat her pregnancy as an experiment, strategically using encryption and a variety of anonymizing techniques to mask her consumer participation in the process of preparing for her baby's birth. Vertesi discussed the difficulty, expense, and resulting anxiety of her decision to avoid revealing her pregnancy to marketers, revealing much about the ubiquity of online tracking and targeted advertising we experience both online and offline.

Resources

Angwin, Julia. 2014. "Has Privacy Become a Luxury Good?" *New York Times*, March 3. Accessed May 30, 2017. https://www.nytimes.com/2014/03/04/opinion/has-privacy-become-a-luxury-good.html .

Faircloth, Kelly. 2014. "Hiding Your Pregnancy from the Internet is Shockingly Difficult." *Jezebel*, April 28. Accessed May 30, 2017. https://jezebel.com/hiding-your-pregnancy-from-the-internet-is-shockingly-d-1568706551 .

Goldstein, Jessica. 2014. "Meet The Woman Who Did Everything In Her Power To Protect Her Pregnancy From Big Data." *ThinkProgress*, April 29. Accessed May 30, 2017. https://thinkprogress.org/meet-the-woman-who-did-everything-in-her-power-to-hide-her-pregnancy-from-big-data-80070cf6edd2

Hess, Amanda. 2017. "How Privacy Became a Commodity for the Rich and Powerful." *New York Times*, May 9. Accessed May

30, 2017. https://www.nytimes.com/2017/05/09/magazine/how-privacy-became-a-commodity-for-the-rich-and-powerful.html .

Hill, Kashmir. 2014. "You Can Hide Your Pregnancy Online, But You'll Feel Like a Criminal." *Forbes*, April 29. Accessed May 30, 2017. https://www.forbes.com/sites/kashmirhill/2014/04/29/you-can-hide-your-pregnancy-online-but-youll-feel-like-a-criminal/#5bc40a6e21f3 .

Petronzio, Matt. 2014. "How One Woman Hid Her Pregnancy From Big Data." *Mashable*, April 26. Accessed May 30, 2017. (includes link to Vertesi's Theorizing the Web conference presentation video) http://mashable.com/2014/04/26/big-data-pregnancy .

Vertesi, Janet. 2014. "My Experiment Opting Out of Big Data Made Me Look Like a Criminal." *Time*, April 30. Accessed May 30, 2017. http://time.com/83200/privacy-internet-big-data-opt-out/ .

Discussion questions

1. Many of the techniques that Vertesi adopted, from using Tor to encrypt online searching to buying gift cards and using cash rather than account-lined payment methods, are associated with criminal behavior rather than privacy. What are some other possible reasons for desiring privacy?

2. Part of Vertesi's experiment involved using gift cards rather than personal credit cards and having online purchases delivered to a locker rather than her home. She noted that many of her techniques to avoid notice were expensive. Does this suggest privacy has the potential to be a luxury good?

3. Vertesi found that data about pregnant women has a value of $1.50 versus ten cents for the average individual. What other groups might be similarly attractive for online marketers? How would they be identified from online behaviors?

4. Vertesi describes a reluctance to engage in social media for fear of inadvertently triggering a conversation about her pregnancy. Were you surprised that social media was a major source of information identifying mothers-to-be?

5. Vertesi went to great lengths to hide a particular and time-limited personal event. Why or why not would such tactics be tenable over the long term? What other life events might inspire a similar need for privacy?

8. ISP consumer data collection

Tyler Hoff

In 2015, the Federal Communications Commission (FCC) ruled that Internet Service Providers (ISPs) were utilities, and therefore under the purview of the FCC rather than the Federal Trade Commission (FTC). In October 2016, the FCC passed privacy regulations banning ISPs from sharing or selling data from consumers without express consent. Congress passed a bill overturning those regulations and preventing the FCC from creating "substantially similar" regulations in the future. On April 3, 2017, President Trump signed the bill into law.

Resources

Brandom, Russell, and Jacob Kastrenakes. 2017. "What Does the New ISP Data-Sharing Rollback Actually Change?" *The Verge*, March 31. Accessed May 30, 2017. http://www.theverge.com/2017/3/31/15138526/isp-privacy-bill-vote-trump-marsha-blackburn-internet-browsing-history .

Brodkin, Jon. 2017. "ISPs and FCC Chair Ajit Pai Celebrate Death of Online Privacy Rules." *Ars Technica*, March 29. Accessed May 30, 2017. https://arstechnica.com/tech-policy/2017/03/isps-and-fcc-chair-ajit-pai-celebrate-death-of-online-privacy-rules/ .

Fung, Brian. 2017. "Trump has Signed Repeal of the FCC Privacy Rules. Here's What Happens Next." *Washington Post*, April 4. Accessed May 30, 2017. https://www.washingtonpost.com/news/the-switch/wp/2017/04/04/trump-has-signed-repeal-of-the-fcc-privacy-rules-heres-what-happens-next/ .

Radia, Ryan. 2017. "Six Reasons FCC Rules Aren't Needed to Protect Privacy." *Competitive Enterprise Institute*, March 27.

Accessed May 30, 2017. https://cei.org/blog/six-reasons-fcc-rules-aren%E2%80%99t-needed-protect-privacy .

Selyukh, Alina. 2017. "As Congress Repeals Internet Privacy Rules, Putting Your Options in Perspective." *NPR*, March 28. Accessed May 30, 2017. http://www.npr.org/sections/alltechconsidered/2017/03/28/521813464/as-congress-repeals-internet-privacy-rules-putting-your-options-in-perspective .

Senate Joint Resolution 34 (the law itself): https://www.congress.gov/115/bills/sjres34/BILLS-115sjres34enr.pdf .

Discussion questions

1. What problem is this law trying to solve? Who benefits? Who does not? What motivated politicians to believe this was a valuable act to benefit the country? Did your elected officials vote for this law? What do you make of their decision?

2. Does this ruling make you want to change your Internet browsing habits? Why or why not? Even without these rules, ISPs are mostly only able to see which websites you visit, not what you do on them. Does this change your opinion?

3. How are these regulations more and less helpful for consumers? Companies? In general?

4. The CEI article argues that the Wiretap Act, which disallows intercepting the contents of electronic communications without consent, also bars ISPs from monitoring metadata, like the websites you visit. Do you agree with this argument? Why or why not?

5. Some ISPs have policies that allow you to opt-out of data collection and sharing, but they are mostly difficult to find and sign up for. Is it worth most consumers' time to opt-out? Why or why not?

6. Can you think of time in history when citizens have shared information that seemed innocuous at the time but ends up having a devastating effect? For example, some people say the data on personal religion gathered by the German government years before Hitler rose to power made it easier to identify Jews later. Do you find this historical reference hyperbolic or prescient?

7. The regulations that were overturned had not yet taken effect. Do you think that overturning these regulations will change how ISPs handle consumer data?

8. The bill was first proposed on March 7, and sent before the Senate on March 15, spending only 8 days up for debate in committee. How do you think this affected the contents of the law?

9. The regulations were overturned using the Congressional Review Act, which allows Congress to pass a resolution of disapproval of a regulation. Congress has passed thirteen such resolutions during the Trump presidency so far, compared to five during the Obama presidency, and just one during the Bush presidency. How does this affect your opinion of Congress and of this law?

9. Encrypted data, privacy, and government access

Jole Seroff

From ancient times, people have used codes, ciphers, wax seals, and other means to disguise information, ensure that no one but the sender has read a document in transit, or verify someone's identity. Today, encryption is used to enable secure communications over the Internet in areas such as online banking and commerce, email, and more. The goal is to protect private information so even if it is intercepted, it will have little value to others.

In addition to private companies' use of encryption software to protect their devices and the data they transmit, millions of individual users of email and messaging services opt to use end-to-end encryption to protect their personal communications from hackers. But some lawmakers argue that encryption software should include an access key for law enforcement.

Consider the sources below to better understand the benefits, risks, and potential legal concerns related to using end-to-end encryption for your digital communications.

Resources

Center for Democracy and Technology. 2016. "Response and Recommendations for the Digital Security Commission Act of 2016." *cdt.org*, May 6. Accessed June 21, 2017. https://cdt.org/insight/response-and-recommendations-for-the-digital-security-commission-act-of-2016/ .

Greenberg, Andy. 2016. "Meet Moxie Marlinspike, The Anarchist Bringing Encryption to All of Us." *Wired*, July 31. Accessed June 21, 2017. https://www.wired.com/2016/07/meet-moxie-marlinspike-anarchist-bringing-encryption-us/ .

Hagemann, Ryan. 2016. "Politics as the Art of the Possible: The McCaul Commission." Niskanen Center, March 1. Accessed June 21, 2017. https://niskanencenter.org/blog/politics-as-the-art-of-the-possible-the-mccaul-commission/ .

"How Encryption Works and How It Can Be Bypassed." 2016. Video file, 2:48. YouTube. Posted by *Wall Street Journal*, March 4. Accessed June 23, 2017. https://www.youtube.com/watch?v=TImdsUglGv4 .

Marlinspike, Moxie. 2013. "Blog: We Should All Have Something to Hide." *Moxie.org*, June 12. Accessed June 21, 2017. https://moxie.org/blog/we-should-all-have-something-to-hide/ .

Pfefferkorn, Riana. 2016. "Here's What the Burr-Feinstein Anti-Crypto Bill Gets Wrong." *Just Security*, April 25. Accessed June 21, 2017. https://www.justsecurity.org/30606/burr-feinstein-crypto-bill-terrible/ .

Senator Dianne Feinstein. 2016. "Intelligence Committee Leaders Release Discussion Draft of Encryption Bill." Press release, April 13. https://www.feinstein.senate.gov/public/index.cfm/2016/4/intelligence-committee-leaders-release-discussion-draft-of-encryption-legislation .

Discussion questions

1. Watch the YouTube video from the *Wall Street Journal* to get a refresher on how end-to-end encryption works. What is encryption? What is its value to society? What are the chal-

lenges it poses for law enforcement? In what ways are these challenges difficult to address?

2. Some feel their messages have no sensitive content and so do not require encryption. Marlinspike's blog post above quotes a law professor and a Supreme Court justice to argue that the complexity of U.S. law makes it nearly impossible to know when one may be in violation of a law or potentially implicated in criminal proceedings. Do you find this or any of Marlinspike's arguments convincing? What, if any, reasons do you see for encrypting personal messages, regardless of their content?

3. In the *Wired* profile of Marlinspike, he is quoted as saying, "I think it should actually be possible to break the law." Part of his argument holds that positive social change requires experimentation with practices outside current norms. Are there other ways for radical ideas to develop into something that could be valuable to mainstream society? Have you ever known of a case in which someone broke a law in a way you thought was justified?

4. While encryption can offer privacy to ordinary citizens, it also offers cover to criminal activity. The Burr-Feinstein bill is intended to require that private companies and individuals comply with court orders to decrypt data for law enforcement purposes. However, much encryption software is developed outside of the U.S., so our laws may not be sufficient to keep encryption out of the hands of criminals. Would you argue that there are still reasons to mandate backdoor access to encrypted devices? Consider the Pfefferkorn source. In your opinion, what are the strongest arguments for or against establishing backdoor access for law enforcement?

5. In the Center for Democracy and Technology (CDT) reading above, CDT rejects the proposal before Congress to establish a National Commission on Security and Technology Challenges. Take a look at the concerns they raise and the recommendations they present. This is a nuanced issue about which much of the public is not well-informed. Imagine you were a reporter crafting a story on this topic. What are some key elements raised in the CDT statement that you would include in your report aiming to better inform the public?

6. The Niskanen Center and the CDT, both organizations that advocate for civil liberties, have distinctly different takes on the proposal to establish a commission to address technology, privacy, and law enforcement, known as the McCaul Commission. Compare and contrast the sources from Niskanen and the CDT. How would you characterize their differences? Do you find one more convincing? Why?

10. Protecting your rights through civic engagement

Tasha Bergson-Michelson

It can be difficult to feel in control when you think about all the ways data is collected and used, both with and without your knowledge or direct consent. In addition to protecting your data through the choices you make about when and how to share it, you have the power to communicate your opinions about how information should be handled directly to your elected officials. Not only can you request that your officials vote for or against a proposed law, but constituents can recommend legislation they would like their officials to sponsor. If you do not believe it is the place of the government to make laws to protect privacy, you can communicate directly to the companies and other organizations that use your data, and use your power as a consumer to advocate for how you would like to see them use, or protect, your data.

Resources

"Contact Your Representatives." n.d. *BeBusinessEd.com*. Accessed June 13, 2017. http://bebusinessed.com/congress-fax-numbers/ . (Learn how to express your opinion to an elected official, a corporation, or another organization.)

Duncan, Geoff. 2014. "Can the Government Regulate Internet Privacy?" *Digital Trends*, April 18. Accessed June 13, 2017. https://www.digitaltrends.com/web/government-warn-us-data-breaches/ .

Kosaka, Glen. 2017. "Is Increased Government Regulation the Answer to Increased Privacy Protection?" *SC Magazine*. Accessed June 13, 2017. https://www.scmagazine.com/is-increased-government-regulation-the-answer-to-increased-privacy-protection/article/557467/ .

"Home." n.d. *Congress.Gov*. Accessed June 13, 2017. https://www.congress.gov/ . (To learn what laws are being proposed, check out in-process bills here.)

"State Laws Related to Internet Privacy." 2017. National Conference of State Legislatures, June 20. Accessed June 23, 2017. http://www.ncsl.org/research/telecommunications-andinformation-technology/state-laws-related-to-internet-privacy.aspx . (To learn the types of laws different states already have in place regarding Internet privacy.)

Taplinger, Susan. 2014. "The Plain Facts: Why Self-Regulation Works Better Than Government Regulation." *DMA*, May 9. Accessed June 13, 2017. https://thedma.org/data-driven-marketing/the-plain-facts-why-self-regulation-works-better-than-government-regulation/ .

Discussion questions

1. Do you think that the government should play a role in protecting consumer data privacy? Why or why not?

2. Do you think that industry self-regulation is an effective way for us to protect personal data? Why or why not?

3. Consider what you have learned about privacy, controlling your personal information, and information ethics. Is there a particular issue about which you feel strongly, either in support of corporate rights to collect and use individual information or about rights of individuals to data privacy?

4. Consider the audience of your letter: an elected official. What kinds of arguments would appeal most to the things that are important to the recipient of your letter? How might you explain why you feel strongly about this particular

topic? Is there some element of your topic that you feel impacts you on a personal level? Why?

5. To whom might you address your concerns? Is it a state-, federal-, or corporate-level concern? Is there a lawmaker, government agency, or business leader for whom your comments would be most pertinent?

6. Today, there are so many ways to communicate. Discuss the advantages or disadvantages of these modes of communication: face-to-face visit, letter, contact on Twitter or Facebook; electronic submission via an elected official's website, fax, or other.

7. Federal elected officials keep offices in their local area as well as in Washington, D.C. Which point of contact might have more effectiveness: one call among many to the nation's capitol or one call among fewer to a regional office?

8. Try crafting a paragraph expressing your opinion to the pertinent recipient.

11. What is a reasonable expectation of privacy?

Jole Seroff

The Fourth Amendment to the Constitution protects citizens from "unreasonable search", but as society changes, what is considered "unreasonable", and as technology advances, is it clear what constitutes a "search"?

Critical precedence was set by the Supreme Court in 1967 in the case of *Katz v. the United States.* Charles Katz was suspected of illegal gambling activities; federal agents attached a listening device on the outside of a public phone booth to capture evidence, but the Supreme Court threw out this evidence, ruling that Katz had a right to expect that his conversation was not being monitored. The agents would have needed to establish probable cause and obtain a warrant to legally record these conversations.

Since 1967 the "reasonable expectation of privacy" has entered our national consciousness, but legally speaking, it's a challenging standard to apply. Importantly, that right is forfeited with regards to information a citizen knowingly shares with a third party, such as an email service or a credit card company. The result is that it may be far from evident which of one's communications are protected. Technological advances further muddy these waters, and new precedents are being set. In *Jones v. United States* (2012), the Supreme Court stated that attaching a GPS device to a car in order to track its movements constituted a search. And in 2014 the court established that a review of suspect's smartphone is a search that requires a warrant, even after a suspect is arrested. (This is as opposed to other contents of an arrestee's pockets, which *can* be searched once an arrest has been made.)

Examine the sources below to consider: How do we establish what is a reasonable expectation of privacy? What new challenges to our definition of privacy are posed by technology? Why are rights to privacy important for our society, even if they may sometimes protect those who are breaking the law?

Resources

Kerr, Orin. 2014. "Answering Justice Alito's Question: What Makes an Expectation of Privacy 'Reasonable'?" *Washington Post*, May 28. Accessed May 27, 2017. https://www.washingtonpost.com/news/volokh-conspiracy/wp/2014/05/28/answering-justice-alitos-question-what-makes-an-expectation-of-privacy-reasonable/ .

Kharpul, Arjun. 2016. "Apple vs FBI: What You Need to Know." *CNBC*, March 8. Accessed May 28, 2017. http://www.cnbc.com/2016/03/29/apple-vs-fbi-all-you-need-to-know.html .

LaChance, Naomi. 2016. "At Supreme Court, Debate over Phone Privacy." NPR, March 8. Accessed May 27, 2017. http://www.npr.org/sections/alltechconsidered/2016/02/29/468609371/at-supreme-court-debate-over-phone-privacy-has-a-long-history .

Selyukh, Alina. 2016. "A Year After San Bernardino and Apple-FBI, Where Are We on Encryption?" *All Tech Considered*. NPR. Dec. 3. Accessed May 27, 2017. http://www.npr.org/sections/alltechconsidered/2016/12/03/504130977/a-year-after-san-bernardino-and-apple-fbi-where-are-we-on-encryption .

Discussion questions

1. Freedom from unwarranted search and the privacy that provides were considered essential values and liberties by the framers of our Constitution. What connections do you see

between legal protection of privacy and the basic principles which underlie our society? In our modern context in which so much is shared publicly, can we understand the value placed on privacy by our founders? Why or why not?

2. One position on privacy holds that those who are not breaking the law have nothing to hide. Does privacy continue to have a valuable role in our lives today? Why or why not?

3. In *United States v. Jones* (2012), Justice Sonia Sotomayor, writing a concurring opinion for the majority, wrote, "Awareness that the Government may be watching chills associational and expressive freedoms. And the Government's unrestrained power to assemble data that reveal private aspects of identity is susceptible to abuse. [It may] alter the relationship between citizen and government in a way that is inimical to democratic society." Do you agree? Why or why not?

4. It is often suggested that we must balance liberties and security; in other words, the more open our society is, the more risk that someone might take advantage of that openness to do something criminal or dangerous. In the majority opinion on *Arizona v. Hicks* (1987), a case often referenced in the Apple and FBI dispute over turning over the phone data of the alleged San Bernardino shooter, Justice Antonin Scalia wrote, "...there is nothing new in the realization that the Constitution sometimes insulates the criminality of a few in order to protect the privacy of us all." Under what circumstances do you think the promise of security is worth the sacrifice of freedoms?

5. In *Riley v. California* and *United States v. Wurie* (both 2014), Chief Justice John Roberts, on behalf of a unanimous decision, wrote, "Modern cell phones are not just another

technological convenience. With all they contain and all they may reveal, they hold for many Americans 'the privacies of life' ... The fact that technology now allows an individual to carry such information in his hand does not make the information any less worthy of the protection for which the Founders fought. Our answer to the question of what police must do before searching a cell phone seized incident to an arrest is accordingly simple — get a warrant." Now that you've read three opinions, how would you define the key aspects of an individual's right to privacy with regard to cell phones?

6. Your rights to privacy only cover content which you have not shared with a third party. Does this knowledge impact the choices you make, for example about what to purchase with a credit card or post on social media? What questions do you ask yourself before posting? How might you help students consider this?

7. Consider the case of *Apple v. FBI* Federal agents asked Apple to override its security software and enable law enforcement access to the San Bernardino shooter Syed Rizwan Farook's iPhone. Apple refused, stating that such a security work-around would set a dangerous precedent encroaching on civil liberties. The suit was dropped when the FBI gained access to the phone with the help of an independent contractor. Would you want the manufacturer of your smartphone to be giving away your personal information?

8. The core dispute is over whether technology companies should be required to build "backdoors" into their software that allow warranted searches. Why might technology companies be unwilling to do so? What is the value of data encryption? Do work-arounds undermine that value?

9. What do you think of the solution that was reached in *Apple v. FBI*? Once there is a search warrant, is it justifiable for U.S. law enforcement to use hacking to gain access to a device locked by encryption? Do you believe that technology companies should be compelled to assist in government access to the devices they produce?

12. Intergenerational differences and data privacy: Generational shift or developmental stage?

Susan Smith

The popular press has suggested that Millennials and their younger siblings, Gen Zs, are relatively cavalier about protecting their data privacy online. But is this accusation really justified? Gen Z (birth years 1996 to present) are *cloud* natives in addition to being digital natives (Center for Intergenerational Kinetics 2016). They have grown up using cell phone apps and social media. More pragmatic and strategic users of social media, Gen Zs have experienced cyberbullying as well as the benefits and celebrity associated with their own content creation. Use of social media is suggested as a key differentiator for Gen Z, who are more concerned about online privacy than Millennials but less so than Gen X and Boomers.

Gen Zers prefer fleeting and anonymous apps like Instagram and Snapchat, and place their trust in social media influencers. They are more likely to share personal information based on the online recommendation of celebrities, organizations, and affinity groups. Controlling for differences in rates of social media use among Boomers, GenXers, and GenZers, data privacy concerns may not be so different. Boomers *say* they are more cautions about sharing personal information, but their online behavior may actually be very similar when on social media. Gen Z seems generally more cautious about most online data requests, but they are willing to share data for more relevant ads. How can educators help them to understand how online "influencers" are leading them to sacrifice data privacy?

Resources

"Data Policy." 2016. *Facebook*, September 29. Accessed June 9, 2017. https://www.facebook.com/about/privacy/ .

Greenblatt, Alan. 2013. "When it Comes to Online Privacy, A Disconnect for the Youth." *NPR*, June 10. Accessed May 30, 2017. http://www.npr.org/sections/alltechconsidered/2013/06/10/190433719/when-it-comes-to-online-privacy-a-disconnect-for-the-young .

Morrison, Nick. 2017. "It's Grades, Not Privacy, that Matter to Generation Z." *Forbes*, January 16. Accessed May 30, 2017. https://www.forbes.com/sites/nickmorrison/2017/01/16/its-grades-not-privacy-that-matter-to-generation-z/#1706cff85d2d .

Murnane, Kevin. 2016. "How Older and Younger Millennials Differ in their Approach to Online Privacy and Security." *Forbes*, April 13. Accessed May 30, 2017. https://www.forbes.com/sites/kevinmurnane/2016/04/13/how-older-and-younger-millennials-differ-in-their-approach-to-online-privacy-and-security/#104c16d39aa3 .

Opsahl, Kurt. 2010. "Facebook's Eroding Privacy Policy: A Timeline." *Electronic Frontier Foundation*, April 28. Accessed May 30, 2017. https://www.eff.org/deeplinks/2010/04/facebook-timeline .

"Privacy Basics." n.d. Facebook. Accessed June 9, 2017. https://www.facebook.com/about/basics .

Stanley, Jay. 2013. "Do Young People Care About Privacy?" *ACLU*, April 29. Accessed May 30, 2017. https://www.aclu.org/blog/do-young-people-care-about-privacy .

Team CGK. 2016. "Online Privacy Expectations Differ Dramatically between Gen Z and Older Generations." *The Center for Generational Kinetics*, February 8. Accessed May 30, 2017. http://genhq.com/online-privacy-expectations-differ-dramatically-between-gen-z-and-older-generations .

Discussion questions

1. How can we explore students' social media and their understanding of data privacy? Develop a lesson plan that either incorporates social media use, or uses scenario-based examples to encourage students to explore what they will share online.

2. How does Gen Z's comfort with online payment apps, like Venmo, change our obligation to teach financial literacy? What are the challenges?

3. How do Gen Z's interests in environmental and social justice causes affect their decisions to share personal information? Have you seen examples of this with school projects or fundraisers for causes they care about?

4. The Murnane article suggests privacy concerns are disregarded when grades or school success are concerned. Do students see the association between apps that track homework habits or reading completion and deeper intrusions into their personal data collection? On a continuum, how do these intrusions rank with data collected on their health and shopping habits?

5. As teachers, discuss your personal privacy concerns as Millennials, Gen Xers or Baby Boomers. On what kinds of apps or online destinations are you most likely to share

information? How might these be shared and used with your students? Do students identify sites that use encryption when profiling users? Do you?

6. If influencers' endorsements convince Gen Zers to trust privacy protections more, ask teens to reflect on their top influencers of the past month. Consider dividing into categories like music, clothing, technology gadgets, etc.

7. If research suggests Gen Z will trade personal data for more targeted ads, how can we help them become more aware of their consumer profile? In other words, when is it worth giving up your data? Do students measure the cost in terms of dollars, products, prestige, prominence, or something else?

8. Review Facebook's privacy changes (see first resource, page 117) from 2005 to 2010 with students, then have them read and review the current policy, using the "Privacy Basics" page for understanding. Review the "Photos" or "Likes and Comments" sections with a discussion group. Which parts of the policy are surprising? Why? If your conversation is a professional development activity with teachers, how might we promote greater understanding of data "leaks" with our students?

13. Comparing United States and European Union approaches to privacy

Jole Seroff

One way to assess the laws and regulations governing the collection and use of data about individuals in the United States is to compare our practices to those of another system. The European Union provides a case study for comparison. Although several factors distinguish the governance of the EU and the U.S., we share many values and democratic practices.

In the U.S., laws have emerged over time to govern specific sectors, such as healthcare or banking. This enables more regulatory flexibility, but can create loopholes or undermine equity in personal data security. In the EU data protection is considered a fundamental right that applies regardless of sector or industry. This creates more uniformity which can simplify implementation, but has also raised concerns around freedom of the press, and critics argue that it stifles business and innovation.

How far is too far to go in protecting individual's rights? What are the differences and the resulting benefits and drawbacks of these two contrasting systems?

Resources

Editorial Board, The. 2015. "Missteps in Europe's Online Privacy Bill." *New York Times*, December 21. Accessed June 6, 2017. https://www.nytimes.com/2015/12/21/opinion/missteps-in-europes-online-privacy-bill.html .

Rouse, Margaret. 2008. "EU Data Protection Directive (Directive 95/46/EC)." *Whatis.com*, January. Accessed June 6, 2017. http://whatis.techtarget.com/definition/EU-Data-Protection-Directive-Directive-95-46-EC .

Scott, Mark and Natasha Singer. 2016. "How Europe Protects Your Online Data Differently Than the U.S." *New York Times*, January 31. Accessed June 6, 2017. https://www.nytimes.com/interactive/2016/01/29/technology/data-privacy-policy-us-europe.html .

Sullivan, Bob. 2006. "U.S. Privacy Laws: EU Citizens Well Protected Against Corporate Intrusion, but Red Tape is Thick." *NBCNews.com*, October 19. Accessed June 6, 2017. http://www.nbcnews.com/id/15221111/ns/technology_and_science-privacy_lost/ .

Toobin, Jeffrey. 2014. "The Solace of Oblivion: In Europe, the right to be forgotten trumps the Internet." *New Yorker*, September 29. Accessed June 6, 2017. http://www.newyorker.com/magazine/2014/09/29/solace-oblivion .

Discussion questions

1. It is often argued that differing attitudes about privacy across the Atlantic can be traced to the events of World War II, when invasion of personal privacy played a pernicious role in totalitarian social control. In the article from *NBCnews.com* above, correspondent Bob Sullivan argues that the divergence in policy between the U.S. and the EU can be traced to another cultural difference: Europeans generally trust government more than corporations; Americans do not, and so do not empower the government to adequately regulate corporate practices with regard to personal data. Do you find either of these arguments compelling? Which do you think sheds more light on our present-day differenc-

es? What other reasons do you see for the variance in our regulatory systems and our attitudes toward personal data privacy?

2. Many EU privacy laws stem from The European Union Directive on Data Protection of 1995, which sets out a basic philosophy privileging privacy. Regulations in the U.S. tend to be industry specific, with different laws applying, for example, to credit card companies than to health care providers. What do you see as the benefits and drawbacks of each of these regulatory approaches?

3. Consider the controversial EU law popularly known as the Right to be Forgotten, by which individuals can file a request with a search engine to eliminate specific results from appearing when someone searches for their name. If private individuals have a right to request that search engines adjust their results, what are the implications for censorship and free access to information? Conversely, is it acceptable that Americans have no recourse with regards to inaccurate or damaging information that might be posted about them without their consent?

4. U.S. privacy regulations are sometimes driven by court cases or action at the state level. For example, the 2003 data breach notification law passed in the state of California requires companies to tell consumers when their personal information has been lost or stolen. Similar laws have subsequently been enacted in other states and have resulted in about 90 million consumer notifications. Given that the U.S. population is estimated at approximately 325 million, 225 million of whom are adults, this means that approximately 40% of adult Americans have been notified of a breach involving their personal data. In your opinion, is the state- or

case-driven model a good one to serve as a basis for U.S. policy? What problems could arise from this approach?

5. Many policies in force at the EU level are not applied uniformly across member nations. Further, some policies are so restrictive that it's common to violate them; consistent enforcement may not be feasible. Considering the challenges of establishing a single policy for multiple nations, what is the value of privacy recommendations at the EU level? Could inconsistent enforcement undermine the integrity of legal guidelines overall?

6. The US and EU have similar regulations designed to protect children. In the US, the Children's Online Privacy Protection Act (COPPA) bans collection of personal data, such as that gathered by social networking sites, from people under 13. Based on your experience either with students or with young people in your personal life, how effective is COPPA? Does it limit exposure of young people to unauthorized data collection? What do you see as the weaknesses of this law? Does it go too far or not far enough? What challenges are inherent in regulating access by age in online spaces?

14. Be strategic! Reading and understanding terms of service and privacy policies

Tasha Bergson-Michelson

Have you ever tried reading a website's privacy policy or terms of service? You know, the one that you click to say that you have read before signing up for a service. According to Pew Research Center, in 2014, 52% of Internet users believed that if a site had a privacy policy that meant the site was keeping user data confidential. In fact, policies may state that anyone using the service gives permission for the owners to access, use, and sell personal data.

But how are we supposed to understand those long, complex, and – let's face it – boring documents? Here are some resources to give you a hand.

Resources

Bailey, Tricia C. n.d. "How to Read a Privacy Policy." Center for Identity at the University of Texas at Austin. Accessed June 21, 2017. https://identity.utexas.edu/id-perspectives/how-to-read-a-privacy-policy .

Center for Identity at the University of Texas at Austin. 2015. "PrivacyCheck Offers Free Tool to Analyze Privacy Policies." *PrivacyCheck*, May 5. Accessed June 24, 2017. https://identity.utexas.edu/press-releases/privacycheck-browser-extension-means-never-reading-a-privacy-policy-again . (Note: The teacher might want to download this extension and demonstrate it for students, or find screenshots online, rather than having each student download the extension in advance.)

Smith, Aaron. 2014. "Half of Online Americans Don't Know What a Privacy Policy Is." *Pew Research Center*, December 4. Accessed June 21, 2017. http://www.pewresearch.org/fact-tank/2014/12/04/half-of-americans-dont-know-what-a-privacy-policy-is/ .

"Terms of Service; Didn't Read." n.d. *Terms of Service; Didn't Read.* Accessed June 21, 2017. https://tosdr.org/ . (Note: This is a crowd-sourced tool; currency may vary.)

Usable Privacy Policy Project. n.d. "Explore Privacy Policies." *Usable Privacy*. Accessed June 21, 2017. https://explore.usableprivacy.org/ .

Wong, Nicole. 2015. "Why I Make My Kids Read Privacy Policies." *Christian Science Monitor*, May 13. Accessed June 21, 2017. https://www.csmonitor.com/World/Passcode/Passcode-Voices/2015/0513/Why-I-make-my-kids-read-privacy-policies .

Discussion questions

1. After reading (and trying out) the resources above, discuss which services you encountered. Make a list in small groups or as a class.

2. What terms of service/privacy policies feel like they are in place to protect you? Do you think they do that well?

3. What terms of service/privacy policies feel like they are in place to benefit the organization at your expense? Why do you feel that way?

4. Which of the terms that benefit the organization more than you do you feel are reasonable, given that you want particular services to exist? Which do you think are invasive or otherwise problematic for the user?

5. Modeled on Bailey's "How to Read a Privacy Policy," make up a list of words you might search for (using control+F or CTRL+F keystrokes on your computer's keyboard) within a privacy policy/terms of service document to protect your own privacy.

6. The resource list above includes numerous tools for helping you understand what is happening with personal information you give to services you use. Which of them do you like best? Why?

7. "Terms of Service; Didn't Read" (ToS;DR) is a crowdsourced tool for helping the public understand terms of service. Because it is crowdsourced (meaning that it relies on volunteer contributions, not scheduled updates by paid staff), it is not always possible to update it immediately when an organization changes its terms. Find the page on ToS;DR for a service you use, and find that organization's terms of service. What needs updating on the ToS;DR website? Create your own document with updated policies for your selected site to share with your class.

15. What does Cambridge Analytica have about you?

Wendy Steadman Stephens

Cambridge Analytica has constructed a database of 230 million American adults, with up to 5,000 pieces of demographic, consumer and lifestyle information for each. Information on file might include any or all of the following:

- voting histories (meaning whether or not you voted; your actual voting decisions are known only to you)
- age
- income
- debt
- hobbies
- criminal history
- purchases and consumer history
- religious leanings
- health concerns
- gun ownership
- car ownership
- home ownership

Supplementing those data points is psychological information users may have shared through quizzes on social media. In both the 2016 Brexit vote and the U.S. presidential election the same year, Cambridge Analytica, a privately-held company, made its data available to campaign organizers to facilitate virtual and geographic microtargeting. In the presidential election, datasets and sophisticated software algorithms were used to place 4,000 differentiated online ads varying in minute detail, including different headings, colors, captions, or which photo or video was shown to a potential voter.

Cambridge Analytica's insights were also used by Trump campaign canvassers on the ground. An app identified the political views and personality types of the inhabitants of a home so that Trump canvassers, prepared with talking points tailored to the resident, only rang at the doors app rated as receptive to his messages.

Highly-targeted marketing played a large role on behalf of conservative candidates and causes in 2016, but it is not exclusive to conservatives. Homegrown data collection systems were developed by the 2008 and 2012 Obama campaigns to help use campaign and fundraising efforts as efficiently and effectively as possible.

Resources

AFP. 2016. "Big Data Helped Trump Even After he Scorned it." *Breitbart*, December 3. Accessed May 30, 2017. http://www.breitbart.com/news/big-data-helped-trump-even-after-he-scorned-it/ .

Bershidsky, Leonid. 2017. "I Want to Surrender to Cambridge Analytica." *Bloomberg*, May 12. Accessed May 30, 2017. https://www.bloomberg.com/view/articles/2017-05-12/i-want-to-surrender-to-cambridge-analytica .

Confessore, Nicholas, and Danny Hakim. 2017. "Data Firm Says 'Secret Suicide' Aided Trump; Many Scoff." *New York Times*, March 6. Accessed May 30, 2017. https://www.nytimes.com/2017/03/06/us/politics/cambridge-analytica.html .

Doward, Jamie, and Alice Gibbs. 2017. "Did Cambridge Analytica Influence the Brexit Vote and the US Election?" *Guardian*, March 4. Accessed May 30, 2017. https://www.theguardian.com/politics/2017/mar/04/nigel-oakes-cambridge-analytica-what-role-brexit-trump .

Funk, McKenzie. 2016. "The Secret Agenda of a Facebook Quiz." *New York Times*, November 19. Accessed May 30, 2017. https://www.nytimes.com/2016/11/20/opinion/the-secret-agenda-of-a-facebook-quiz.html .

Grassegger, Hannes, and Mikael Krogerus. 2017. "The Data that Turned the World Upside Down." *Vice*, January 28. Accessed May 30, 2017. https://motherboard.vice.com/en_us/article/big-data-cambridge-analytica-brexit-trump .

Kosinski, Michal, David Stillwell, and Thore Graepel. 2013. "Private traits and attributes are predictable from digital records of human behavior." *Proceeding of the National Academy of Sciences 110* (15) 5802-5805; doi:10.1073/pnas.1218772110 .

Discussion questions

1. The U.K. and Europe have strict privacy protections limiting the use of personal information, but U.S. data brokers have both broad access to local and state government records and to troves of consumer information available to any company or candidate who can afford them. Who might each approach benefit?

2. Cambridge Analytica treats data points it has collected as proprietary information, voicing reluctance to reveal specifics in case its intellectual property is reverse-engineered. However, it has provided examples including mapping the

types of music an individual listens to on Pandora to those using a particular Snapchat filter. What are some ways you can avoid cross-platform tracking?

3. On the basis of an average of 68 Facebook "likes" by a user, it was possible to predict their race (95% accuracy), sexual orientation (88% accuracy), and Democratic or Republican party affiliation (85% accuracy) (Kosinski, Stillwell & Graepel, 2013). Will this change the way you interact with social networks?

4. Cambridge Analytica's model relies upon the OCEAN theory of personality — openness, conscientiousness, extroversion, agreeableness, and neuroticism. Are those traits static or could they change over time? Are there other traits that you think would help Cambridge Analytica better know a consumer?

5. How could your quality of life could improve by allowing companies to better tailor the communications you receive?

6. According to the U.S. Census Bureau (census.gov/quickfacts), there were approximately 234 million adults in the United States in 2014. How does knowing that statistical benchmark help you gain understanding of the number of citizen profiles Cambridge Analytica has (approximately 230 million)? How does that knowledge change or reinforce your opinions on Cambridge Analytica's scope or practices?

7. Cambridge Analytica will sell its data, but the data is expensive. What impact might its data have on an election in which a very wealthy, well-funded candidate who can afford Cambridge Analytica's data is pitched against one with fewer financial means?

CITIZEN SCIENCE

1. Scientists and citizen scientists: Cooperation and reservations.......................132

2. Candy Crush and Zooniverse: The psychology of citizen science 135

3. Citizen science techniques to uncover insights in the humanities.................139

4. Tour of the Leafsnap leaf identification app..142

5. Habitat Network: Learningabout and managing the landscape we share..145

6. Smithsonian Institution Transcription Center 148

7. Where does federal data go? 151

8. Native knowledge meets scientific knowledge through citizen science 155

1. Scientists and citizen scientists: Cooperation and reservations

Kelly Hovinga

Citizen science projects engage people — often with little formal scientific training — in collecting, analyzing, and/or tagging data about the natural world. Interactions can occur in nature, such as counting birds, looking for tags on butterflies, or banding turtles. With increasing frequency, citizen scientist projects can be completed via online project portals, allowing armchair astronomers to look for galaxy patterns, amateur biologists to tag elephants in photographs, and non-professional medical researchers to outline the nucleus of cells.

These volunteer labors are often under the direction of a professional scientist, who may design the research study or even take the volunteers' raw data and process and synthesize it. Given that funding for research is highly competitive in the sciences, citizen science contributions can dramatically accelerate the quantity and speed of the research process. More can be done with fewer funds.

While citizen science can yield important results, how are citizen scientists viewed by the professionals with years of formal training? Here, we'll look at three citizen science projects as well as a scientist's analysis of a citizen scientist project. The first project is River Keeping, the second is online browsing history, and the third is roadkill. The scientist's editorial discusses the recent concern over artificial turf causing cancer.

Resources

Meyer, Chelsey. 2017. "Citizen Scientists Donate Data for Online Price Personalization Research." *Discover*, May 3. Accessed June 9, 2017. http://blogs.discovermagazine.com/citizen-science-salon/2017/05/03/citizen-scientists-donate-data-for-online-price-personalization-research/#.WTqsyuvyvIV .

Ropeik, David. 2017. "Citizen science often overstates 'cancer clusters' like the one linked to artificial turf." *Stat*, May 5. Accessed June 9, 2017. https://www.statnews.com/2017/05/05/cancer-clusters-artificial-turf/ .

Russell, Sharman. 2017. "River Keeping in New Mexico." *Discover*, April 25. Accessed June 9, 2017. http://blogs.discovermagazine.com/citizen-science-salon/2017/04/25/river-keeping-in-new-mexico/#.WRNX7PnyvIU .

Strickland, Eliza. 2010. "Citizen Scientists Take Charge of California's Roadkill." *Discover*, September 14. Accessed June 9, 2016. http://blogs.discovermagazine.com/discoblog/2010/09/14/citizen-scientists-take-charge-of-californias-roadkill/#.WTqtNOvyvIV .

Discussion questions

1. How do the various citizen scientists contribute to research in these articles? What does their involvement make possible that might not otherwise be possible?

2. What previous training is required and is not required to be a citizen scientist in these examples?

3. How do the various authors view citizen scientists? Do they

mention any citizen scientists by name? How do they use language to describe these citizen scientists?

4. What are the scientists asking citizen scientists to do? Who should be credited when new findings are discovered?

5. What are some of the possible limitations with citizen science and with using volunteer efforts in general?

6. David Ropeik says, "Citizen epidemiology can be tremendously valuable, but it is not science." Do you agree with this statement? Why?

7. One hundred years ago and more, the distinction between formal and informal science investigations was significantly blurrier than it is today. It was considered appropriate for upper-class gentlemen to engage in the study and classification of insects, flowers, and animals, for example. Doctoral degrees were far less common than today. How has science changed as a result? Has anything been lost?

8. How is the study that Griffin conducted in the *Stat* article different than the studies conducted by citizen scientists in the other articles? Why might that matter?

9. Why might the authors from *Discover* choose to write about citizen science in a very positive light?

10. Why might Ropeik write about citizen science in a negative light?

11. After looking through the articles, what kind of research benefits from citizen science? Should citizen scientists try to move beyond those expectations? Why or why not?

2. Candy Crush and Zooniverse: The psychology of citizen science

Kelly Hovinga

My father handed me his binoculars as we stood amidst the tall grass. Through the lenses, I watched the controversial reintroduction of wolves into Yellowstone National Park. I was only five, but to this day I remember fuzzy dots running through the arid foothills of Western Montana. Years later, I defended species reintroduction in a debate during social studies class. Oftentimes, the act of seeing a living animal at a young age has an impact on how children evaluate the value of wildlife (Clayton n.d.). Citizen science projects like Zooniverse allow children and adults to view pictures of animals in the wild, helping both with the conservation of animals and the fostering of appreciation for wildlife.

Many citizen science projects have turned to the human processing power for pattern recognition in the classification and sorting of data. At first blush, the act of looking at picture after picture seems like it would be mind-numbing; however, the citizen science projects that utilize this method have proven to be very popular and effective ... and keep volunteers' attention. The success of Zooniverse's methodology has to do with psychological imperatives built into the human brain regarding pattern recognition and community building.

Take, for example, Wildwatch Kenya, a citizen science project on the Zooniverse.org platform that focuses on giraffes and other vulnerable or endangered species. Researchers have rigged 100 cameras with motion sensors along trails in the nature preserves of Kenya. Every day, the cameras take thousands of pictures and upload them. Volunteer classifiers are "served up" one random image at a time and are asked to identify the animals in the picture. To maximize accuracy among these non-zoologist participants, each picture is sent to fifteen participants. The reality is that while artificial intelligence (AI) can identify many things, humans can still do a better job. Researchers use the resulting tagged images to verify the existence of new species of giraffes, track giraffe migratory habits and activities, and document other species that share their habitats. Scientists hope this data and the conclusions derived from it will contribute to the preservation and conservation of giraffes and their environment.

Is it just cute mammals that keep volunteers at their computers? Perhaps there's more to it than that — perhaps the same instincts that keep us engaged with animal identification projects like Wildwatch Kenya, Michigan Zoomin, Penguin Watch, or Elephant Expedition (all on Zooniverse.org) is similar to the psychological effects of playing repetitive games like Candy Crush, Tetris, or Bejeweled.

This case study looks at the psychology behind environmental citizen science projects that rely on pattern recognition and how these projects foster conservation concerns within the participants. Before reading the articles and discussion questions below, please spend fifteen minutes or so actually participating in the citizen science project (link here: https://www.zooniverse.org/projects/sandiegozooglobal/wildwatch-kenya). While you can participate without logging in, creating an account will let you keep track of your citizen science efforts across time.

Resources

Clayton, Susan. n.d. "Learning to Care About Animal Conservation." *Center for Humans & Nature*. Accessed July 21, 2017. http://www.humansandnature.org/learning-to-care-about-animal-conservation .

Dockterman, Eliana. 2013. "Candy Crush Saga: The Science Behind Our Addiction." *Time,* November 15. Accessed July 21, 2017. http://business.time.com/2013/11/15/candy-crush-saga-the-science-behind-our-addiction/ .

Hillman, Keith. 2016. "Pattern Recognition and Your Brain." *Psychology24*, March 21. Accessed July 21, 2017. http://www.psychology24.org/pattern-recognition-and-your-brain/ .

Stafford, Tom. 2012. "The Psychology of Tetris." *BBC,* October 23. Accessed July 21, 2017. http://www.bbc.com/future/story/20121022-the-psychology-of-tetris .

Zooniverse.org. n.d. "Projects." Accessed September 13, 2017. http:/zooniverse.org/projects . (Search for Wildwatch Kenya so you can explore it before continuing with the discussion questions.)

Discussion questions

1. When you were exploring Wildwatch Kenya, did you have questions afterward about the animals in the photographs? For example, did observing animals at night or seeing animals in clusters versus alone raise new lines of inquiry? How did you feel when the picture showed an animal you had never seen in the wild before?

2. Do you think the potential spike in dopamine caused by a successful recognition affected how long you persevered with the animal identification task?

3. What are some of the similarities and differences you noticed between the games Candy Crush, Bejeweled, and Tetris and the act of identifying animals on Zooniverse?

4. Think about the steps you took to identify an animal that might not have been instantly recognizable. How did you go about trying to identify it? Do you see pattern recognition activity in your decision-making?

5. How big of an influence do you think psychological factors play in the retention of Zooniverse volunteers? What might be other reasons why people return to the site?

6. The first pop-up on the Classify page for Wildwatch Kenya says, "In many cases, you'll be one of the first to see [the pictures]!" Do you believe this influences how you feel about the process and the animals in the pictures? Why or why not?

7. Do you think you would feel differently about the experience if you were looking at animals native to your location instead of animals in Africa? Why or why not?

8. What studies would you like to see conducted on the psychological impacts of online citizen science identification projects?

9. Did you end up using the chat option to go to the forums to discuss what you saw? If you did, what did you notice about the conversations? How does that fit into social psychology?

10. Do you think you will do this again? Is the use of game mentality an ethical method in citizen science projects? Why or why not?

3. Citizen science techniques to uncover insights in the humanities

Connie Williams

Even though "citizen science" appears, from its name, to be only about science, nothing could be further from the truth. Utilizing the skills, observation and intent of citizen science projects – those projects that include citizen participation in the capturing, interpreting, and analyzing of data – encompass a wide variety of subject areas including art, history, biography, and government.

Artist sketchbooks and diaries can enlighten art enthusiasts, while reviewing old sailor logbooks and transcribing Civil War soldier diaries help us to understand the daily lives of previous generations and their unique perspectives. At the same time, the work of transcribing the content of these documents makes the information collected available for study and understanding. These projects help students to see data differently: Not just as a series of tick marks or numbers but as snippets from a past world that, together, form an intriguing constellation of ideas, thoughts and perceptions. By crowdsourcing the efforts of many enthusiastic volunteers, new insights emerge as well.

Projects on the Zooniverse.org citizen science portal cross many subject areas from biology, physics, and ecology to humanities-based subjects such as language, literature, art, and history. Many of these include transcription of letters, diaries or other hand-written documents. Students have much to gain by joining in on projects like these because they gain an uncommon perspective: the ability to see the world via the minutia of one person's daily observations. As they engage with projects to transcribe and describe primary source documents into text that can be easily searched by future scholars, students can see how someone living in a different time and place observed his or her world. Historians on the back end of the project gain a collection of documents that are easy to use, thereby giving them access to a wider view of their research.

How can we create a classroom environment that encourages students to notice how these documents and artifacts are data points? And when those data points become scannable and searchable, how can students see that the affordances of current technologies can give us new insights into the past? How can humanities-based citizen science projects help students to walk in the footsteps of others to see what drives their collaboration, discovery, and innovation?

In this case study, we invite you to divide the participants up into small groups. Give each group a project you've selected in advance from Zooniverse.org/projects from the Arts, History, Language, Literature, or Social Science categories. Then invite them to share what they have learned, brainstorm teaching and learning connections, and respond to the questions below.

Resources

Zooniverse.org. n.d. "Projects." Accessed June 30, 2017. http://zooniverse.org/projects .

Discussion questions

1. How might humanities data collection differ from more typical definitions of citizen science data collection?

2. What questions might one ask of an historical document that they might not ask of a scientific document?

3. If there are lots of documents in museums and other archives, how might digitizing them help us with access? What can we gain from this access?

4. How can humanities subject specialists learn from data gathered by projects like those available in the Zooniverse categories listed above?

5. How can the humanities use citizen science data to gain a deeper understanding of culture? How does crowdsourcing the effort impact this understanding?

6. What can the humanities learn about research from the citizen science movement so that they can apply it to their own subject?

7. Why would a K-12 teacher engage students with a humanities-based citizen science project?

8. Once a teacher has completed a unit using a citizen science project, how could he/she bring it together for students to see/understand the bigger context/picture of their work?

9. What would assessment look like for participation in a humanities-based citizen science project?

4. Tour of the Leafsnap leaf identification app

Wendy Steadman Stephens

Leafsnap is an online database with a mobile app interface for tree identification, providing high-resolution images of trees' flowers, fruits, petioles, seeds, and bark along with their known geographic distribution. An image import feature allows users to tag images with geocoded location data, contributing to mapping and monitoring biodiversity in the Plant kingdom.

The mobile app uses the device camera to capture visual information about the edges and contours of the leaf to compare to its database. The app processes the image to suggest possible genus and species, but relies upon the user to refine the results. When users upload or import their own photographs, the app encodes them with location information in the form of geospatial data. This encoding automatically links the photo information to the location and adjusts the mapped range of the species as necessary.

The web-based version features tabs for Northeast US, New York, Washington, D.C., and Canada; an independent U.K. version is supported by the Natural History Museum in London. An alphabetically sorted list has columns for leaf, flower, fruit, common and scientific names. The more than 20,000 high-quality laboratory images from the Smithsonian collection appear in controlled backlit and front-lit versions, with several samples per species on black backgrounds for contrast. In addition, more than 7,000 images have been uploaded from the field, taken by mobile devices in outdoor environments containing varying amounts of blur, light, and shadow. The dataset is also available for research.

In this case study, you'll explore Leafsnap and its algorithms to consider potential possible influences that could affect the app's database.

Resources

Kumar, Neeraj. 2012. "Leafsnap: An Electronic Field Guide." Neeraj Kumar. Accessed May 30, 2017. http://neerajkumar.org/projects/leafsnap/ .

Marx, Eric. 2011. "LeafSnap, the Field Guide on Your iPhone." *Popular Mechanics*, July 13. Accessed May 30, 2017. http://www.popularmechanics.com/technology/gadgets/reviews/a6938/leafsnap-the-field-guide-on-your-iphone/ .

Stephens, Wendy. 2014. "App of the Week: LeafSnap." *YALSA Blog*, July 30. Accessed May 30, 2017. http://yalsa.ala.org/blog/2014/07/30/app-of-the-week-leafsnap/ .

"Unifying Life Site: Placing Urban Tree Diversity in an Evolutionary Context." n.d. City College of New York. Accessed June 8, 2017. https://www.ccny.cuny.edu/education/unifying_life_site .

Discussion questions

1. The Leafsnap project started in the Northeast United States with Columbia University, the University of Maryland, and the Smithsonian Institution as founding partners, with plans to expand to include the whole of the United States. What is the relationship between this area's dense population, early settlement, and tree data? Do you think the app could be useful in other geographic areas? Rural areas?

2. The dynamic nature of the Leafsnap database makes it a modern update to traditional printed field guides. What features are unique to its digital incarnation?

3. Leafsnap got its start in facial recognition software. Thinking about the capabilities of augmented reality apps like Google Translate and Aurasma, what else might be identifiable by shape?

4. Given the high resolution camera necessary to submit images, who do you think contributes to Leafsnap? Do you think mobile computing can be democratizing in this context? Why or why not?

5. Habitat Network: Learning about and managing the landscape we share

Susan D. Ballard

Originally begun in 2012 as the YardMap project, the Habitat Network is associated with the Cornell University Lab of Ornithology and the Nature Conservancy as a platform for citizen science. Habitat Network provides an opportunity for individuals, including members of the professional science community and ordinary citizens to collaborate and share information in order to develop a better and deeper understanding of the environments we share with wildlife. Data is collected as individuals across the country create an account and "draw maps of their backyards, parks, farms, favorite birding locations, schools, and gardens" (Habitat Network 2017). The project is designed to provide participants with landscape details and tools so that they learn how to manage and sustain wildlife habitats as part of a greater conservation community.

The project relies upon a three-part process:

- » **Draw a map** (to assess the habitat);
- » **Learn about habitat** (use custom tools and articles to create habitat and seek out guidance from the community);
- » **Create change** (use information to manage the habitat; report back on changes made and impact).

The Explore Tab provides:

- » an opportunity to **enter a ZIP code and discover local resources** such as information about the particular EcoRegion, pollinators, native plants, and local experts;

- » a link to a **photo gallery** of images submitted by participants;
- » a **graphic representation** of the "average" American backyard; and
- » featured sites of **exemplary projects**.

The Learn tab provides menu-driven access to vetted and linked articles on native plants, healthy ecosystems, design advice, flora and fauna, mapping, and more.

In this case study, you'll explore some background information about biodiversity, the Habitat Network site itself, and the website for the lead organizations behind Habitat Network. Then you'll discuss how this site might be a useful citizen science site for your community.

Resources

Bies, Laura. 2014. "Wildlife Habitat Fragmentation Fact Sheet." The Wildlife Society. Accessed July 10, 2017. wildlife.org/wp-content/uploads/2014/05/Wildlife-Habitat-Fragmentation.pdf .

"Habitat Network." 2017. Cornell Lab of Ornithology. Accessed July 11, 2017. http://content.yardmap.org .

"Home Page." 2017. Cornell Lab of Ornithology. Accessed July 11, 2017. http://www.birds.cornell.edu/Page.aspx?pid=1478 .

"Home Page." 2017. Nature Conservancy. Accessed September 13, 2017. https://www.nature.org .

"What is Biodiversity?" n.d. National Wildlife Federation. Accessed July 10, 2017. http://www.nwf.org/Wildlife/Wildlife-Conservation/Biodiversity.aspx .

Discussion questions

1. Why is it important to study and share practices to improve the wildlife value of residential landscapes? Does your answer change if you live in a rural, urban, or suburban area? Why or why not?

2. Observational studies such as the Habitat Network have limitations that "gold standard" research projects may not have. For example, they may lack of rigorous controls, replication, randomization, or baseline data. Why is crowdsourced observation still valuable?

3. Does transforming urban areas into functional habitat to better support a diversity of wildlife also increase the quality of life for people and communities? Why or why not?

4. Thinking about your own community, have you noticed any changes, good or bad, impacting wildlife habitat? What are the consequences, both positive and negative?

5. Can you identify an area in your community that has been impacted recently by habitat fragmentation? How might the community mitigate the impact?

6. What other types of data collection do you think would be useful to assess habitats and wildlife health in your community?

7. Go online and look at the websites for the Cornell Lab of Ornithology and the Nature Conservancy. Are there other projects that your community and/or school might be interested in participating in?

8. How can activists further promote engagement with habitat conservation efforts?

6. Smithsonian Institution Transcription Center

Tyler Hoff

There are many projects on the Internet taking advantage of crowdsourcing to speed up and validate laborious and painstaking tasks. One of these projects is the Smithsonian Transcription Center (http://transcription.si.edu), which allows volunteers to sign up and help to transcribe analog texts given to the Smithsonian for online access. These range from scientific journals to diaries from explorers to jokes from Phyllis Diller's personal joke collection. While the material varies broadly, the common thread is that the text is such that a computer cannot properly scan it, hence the need for volunteers. Anyone may sign up to be a volunteer (or, as they like to say, volun*peers*), and there is no minimum requirement for time worked or expertise. Multiple rounds of transcription help staff and volunteers alike feel confident that accuracy will be developed over time.

Resources

Smithsonian Digital Volunteers: Description Center. 2017. "About." *Smithsonian Institution*. Accessed September 13, 2017. https://transcription.si.edu/about .

Smithsonian Digital Volunteers: Description Center. 2017. "Tips." *Smithsonian Institution*. Accessed September 13, 2017. https://transcription.si.edu/tips .

Wright, Andy. 2016. "How the Smithsonian Institution is Crowdsourcing History." *Atlas Obscura*, February 10. Accessed May 30, 2017. http://www.atlasobscura.com/articles/how-the-smithsonian-is-crowdsourcing-history .

For the rest of this activity, we recommend you give participants at least 20 minutes to make an account, explore the site and its projects, and try their hand at transcribing a document to see what they can discover.

Discussion questions

1. What general similarities or differences do you notice between the projects? How do they connect to your curriculum, service club volunteer needs, or community interests?

2. What subject matters were covered in the projects you saw? Did you feel like most subject areas were covered by the selected projects? What factors do you think went into choosing specific projects for the Transcription Center?

3. From the projects you saw, do you think you are equipped to participate right now? If not, what expertise or training would you need to feel like you could participate effectively? Even if you feel ready to participate, what training could the Smithsonian provide that would improve the contributions of the volunteers?

4. Does this project appeal to a particular subset of society, by education or socioeconomic class? Why? What could be done to appeal to a broader swath of society?

5. Most of the Smithsonian collection is handwritten, and much of that is in cursive. How does that impact what volunteers are interested and equipped to help in a substantive way?

6. What impact does being hosted by the Smithsonian have on the appeal of the projects? The contents? Funding?

7. How easy to use is the website? Do you think it encourages people to get involved, and does it make it easy for them to do so?

8. What barriers are there for other museums and archival institutions to engage in the same kind of project?

9. Which projects were particularly compelling to you? Which were not? Were there any that you feel no one would be interested in?

10. What could the Smithsonian do to encourage participation in specific projects? Should it do so?

11. Do you think some of these projects are more worthy of inclusion than others? Discuss why you may or may not think some are more or less worthy, and what selection criteria the Smithsonian should use in the future.

7. Where does federal data go?

Connie Williams

A government document is any document produced by the government with taxpayer money. With rare exceptions, government documents are not protected by copyright; instead, they are considered to be in the *public domain*, meaning that they belong to all of us. Some government information is mandated, with direct legal instruction to compile data, or provide proof of service or collect particular information. Government information is an ever-changing commodity subject to politics, economics, and legalities. In the past, government documents would be printed on paper and sent out to a variety of government document repositories that would collect, catalog, and make these documents available to researchers and the public. If a report went out of print or if government priorities changed, those documents remained in those print collections.

As the government has continued to publish its documents online, at great cost savings over print production, it has emerged that there is no formal requirement for federal agencies to archive their online content at the federal level. Therefore, some online government information is archived, but some is vulnerable to loss.

Government websites change with each new presidential administration, and efforts to build archival systems have been underway for nearly a decade. As early as 2008, the End of Term Web Archive project of the California Digital Library and the Internet Archive were working to copy and archive government websites at the end of a presidential administration (see http://eotarchive.cdlib.org/). With the addition of the Library of Congress, University of North Texas Libraries, George Washington University Libraries, Stanford University Libraries, and the U.S.

Government Publishing Office, the project grew into the End of Term Presidential Harvest, which began saving online government content in July 2016, months before the November 2016 presidential election outcome was known (see http://digital2.library.unt.edu/nomination/eth2016/about/).

However, with the 2017 presidential transition, government information has been scrutinized carefully by the new administration for political position and viewpoint. There is a concern among citizens that access to historical government data will be closed, and new data will remain secreted behind closed Agency doors. There is also uncertainty about the preservation of data if government agencies are defunded and closed moving forward.

The Open Government Act (https://www.congress.gov/bill/115th-congress/house-bill/1770) has been proposed to keep public Agency information open and available for citizens to see and use. If passed, each Agency would create and follow an "Open Government Plan" and post it on their websites.

Many are worried that important government information not only will be, but is, being lost. What are the ramifications of these changes? Who owns the data once it is no longer accessible? In this case study, you'll browse the sites below to gain awareness of the issues around archiving and accessing government data.

Resources

Cornell University Library. 2017. "A Guide to International and US Statistics Sources: Archived Government Data," June 13. Cornell University. Accessed July 7, 2017. http://guides.library.cornell.edu/datasources/archived_gov_data .

DataRefuge. n.d. "Data Refuge: Building Refuge for Federal Climate & Environmental Data." Accessed July 7, 2017. http://www.datarefuge.org .

California Digital Library, Internet Archive. "Home." End of Term Web Archive. Accessed July 7, 2017. http://eotarchive.cdlib.org/ .

Dwyer, Jim. 2016. "Harvesting Government History, One Web Page at a Time." *The New York Times*, December 1. Accessed July 7, 2017. https://www.nytimes.com/2016/12/01/nyregion/harvesting-government-history-one-web-page-at-a-time.html .

Eilperin, Juliet. 2017. "Under Trump, Inconvenient Data is Being Sidelined." *Washington Post*, May 14. Accessed July 7, 2017. http://wapo.st/2pL2YtN .

"Index." 2014. Internet Archive: Wayback Machine, December 31. Accessed July 7, 2017. https://archive.org/web/ .

Jefferson. 2016. "Preserving U.S. Government Websites and Data as the Obama Term Ends." Internet Archive Blogs, December 15. Accessed September 13, 2017. http://blog.archive.org/2016/12/15/preserving-u-s-government-websites-and-data-as-the-obama-term-ends/ .

Mooney, Chris and Juliet Eilperin. 2017. "EPA Website Removes Climate Science Site From Public View After Two Decades." *The Washington Post*, April 29. Accessed July 7, 2017. https://www.washingtonpost.com/news/energy-environment/wp/2017/04/28/epa-website-removes-climate-science-site-from-public-view-after-two-decades/ .

Discussion questions

1. Who owns government data and who should determine who can access it?

2. Who benefits from being able to access government data? Who benefits when data disappears? What right do ordinary

citizens have to accessing government data? Who should decide?

3. How would you go about finding government datasets? Who would you ask for assistance?

4. Which projects seem to have the most promising capabilities to preserve government data? Which strategies do you find most compelling? Most valuable?

5. Some government datasets, such as citizen science projects hosted by the National Oceanic and Atmospheric Administration (NOAA), the National Aeronautics and Space Administration (NASA), and the Smithsonian Institution (SI), is constructed with data provided by ordinary citizens who believe they are contributing to a more effective and impactful government. What rights do citizens have to be able to access datasets to which they have contributed?

6. Since websites change with different administrations, where does the previous administration's information go?

7. Do you see datasets as objective or subjective? Is government information authoritative, if it can come and go at will?

8. Native knowledge meets scientific knowledge through citizen science

Connie Williams

Long before Western explorers discovered that there were lands and peoples living beyond their own world, these people were traveling across oceans, navigating from island to island and other land forms with knowledge acquired by experience, education, and lore. Ancient Pacific Islanders could navigate between landforms by reading waves, wind, and bird patterns. Inuit weather predictors relied also on the visual, physical, and observational patterns of wind, cloud formations and other clues to upcoming weather (CU Boulder Today 2010).

Today, weather forecasters use the power of the Big Data of the historical record alongside worldwide contemporary observations to predict the next round of heat or in-coming storms. Yet, even with the help of immense data, has weather forecasting become more accurate today than in previous generations?

"Native knowledge" – that knowledge handed down through generations by direct instruction, storytelling, cultural folklore, and daily observation – provides a kind of knowledge gleaned from decades of informal and personal data collection that has worked previously, but may or may not be grounded in scientific research. Yet for centuries, it has been used to guide people through processes (such as weather, birth, health, farming, and gardening) that impact our lives. Such knowledge helps us create a sense of understanding around which we create our social, legal, and cultural norms.

What some scientists call "alternative knowledge" can be considered as knowledge that is derived from sources other than those conducted scientifically, e.g., "ancient wisdom." "Old wives' tales" fit into this category, as most of us have benefitted from [much to our chagrin sometimes] the advice handed down to us from our mothers and grandmothers. There are many examples of scientific research designed to prove or disprove the substance of motherly claims.

Which data should we trust: lived data, scientifically-gathered data according to Western principles, or both?

Resources

Arctic Eider Society. n.d. IK-MAP. Accessed August 1, 2017. https://arcticeider.com/map .

"Comparisons Between Traditional & Scientific Knowledge." n.d. Alaska Native Science Commission. Accessed July 7, 2017. http://www.nativescience.org/html/traditional_and_scientific.html .

"How to Make an Igloo." Created by Craig S. Smith, Kaitlyn Mullin, and Maureen Towey. *New York Times*, 2017. Accessed July 24, 2017. https://www.nytimes.com/video/world/canada/100000004999377/how-to-build-an-igloo.html .

Kestler-D'amours, Jillian. 2017. "Introducing an Online Encyclopedia of Inuit Arctic Observations." *NewsDeeply*, April 20. Accessed August 1, 2017. https://www.newsdeeply.com/arctic/articles/2017/04/20/introducing-an-online-encyclopedia-of-inuit-arctic-observations .

Ocean Today, NOAA. n.d. "The Ocean Shows Us the Way." Video, 1:50. Accessed July 7, 2017. http://oceantoday.noaa.gov/oceanshowsusway/ .

Stillman, Janice. 2013. "History of the *Old Farmer's Almanac*: The Almanac Editors' Legacies." *The Old Farmer's Almanac*. Accessed July 7, 2017. http://www.almanac.com/content/history-old-farmers-almanac .

Strategic Relations. 2010. "Traditional Inuit Knowledge Combines With Science to Shape Arctic Weather Insights." *CU Boulder Today*, April 7. Accessed July 7, 2017. http://www.colorado.edu/today/2010/04/07/traditional-inuit-knowledge-combines-science-shape-arctic-weather-insights .

Discussion questions

1. Begin by viewing the *New York Times* video on creating an igloo. What kinds of knowledge do you see playing out in the video? How might a formally-trained scientist explain what is happening?

2. How does native knowledge, which thrives on observation based on daily impacts compare to the data captured by citizen scientists, which is built on quick observation of empirical data?

3. Consider the Kestler-D'Amours article and the IK-MAP project. How does this project show a partnership between contemporary data documentation methods used by scientific experts with the deep traditional knowledge of elders?

4. *The Farmer's Almanac* was first published in 1792, bringing data and observational lore to farmers, sailors, and city dwellers. How might a publication like this kick-start scientific observation – not expensive and sophisticated data collection tools – as a way to predict upcoming weather, how to best plant our garden, and when to head to the river to fish?

5. How might knowledge accumulated through the years or generations and through social connections be construed as citizen science? Are they similar in any way?

6. Are "old wives' tales" considered to be incorrect because of implied sexism? For example, does society downplay these tips because of an inherent bias that knowledge handed down from women cannot be factual? What other "tales" are discounted because they do not come from scientific evidence?

7. How has science interrupted native knowledge, bringing about unhealthy or unsafe processes?

8. How might native processes – those rituals and/or solutions used by those within a cultural context – have interrupted science by refusing to make important changes?

9. How can indigenous knowledge work with Big Data to create new solutions to problems? What examples do you see in the readings above?

10. How might scientific research help native knowledge recognize changing patterns that might not be easily seen in the short time periods within its changes?

Bonus feature: Choosing a citizen science project for your classroom

Susan Smith, with Connie Williams, and Debbie Abilock

Citizen science (we call it C-science) projects offer teachers the opportunity to connect their students to scientists doing real research on real-world problems. Some citizen science projects help students engage with the natural world: counting butterflies in a field, using telescopes to scan the night sky, photographing mosquitos, or measuring photosynthesis. Others involve online contributions, like marking up images of cells, counting penguins, pinpointing the eye of the storm on radar images, and identifying wildlife in photos. There are even projects on citizen science sites that use C-science principles of collaboration and crowdsourcing to look more closely into art, history, or culture, but aren't science at all — such as transcribing Civil War telegrams, Phyllis Diller's joke file, and tagging images so scholars can search and find relevant graphics in less time. These "citizen humanities" projects follow the same format and mission as C-science, but encourage citizens to interact with artifacts including letters, diaries, documents, and images.

Done well, C-science can make science "come alive" for students, by connecting them to the scientific community at large, encouraging them to engage with the global community and empowering them to design their own research that might open new insights about the world around them. How do we find the "right" project for our students and our courses? There is no Match.com for teachers and projects; however, there are some considerations that can help you plan a rich and rewarding experience for you and your students.

What is citizen science?

While citizens have done this for centuries, the modern idea of a citizen scientist emerged from increasingly large, professionalized scientific research projects in the 1900s. The earliest C-science projects were often driven by the need for geographically diverse data or by scientists looking to scale data collection beyond what they could accomplish on their own. Today, there are C-science projects led by scientists in universities, activist-scientists working at non-profit organizations, even neighbor-to-neighbor grass-roots initiatives. In fact, some of today's longest-running citizen science projects were born out of the activist movement of the 1960's — ordinary citizens taking action to improve the world around them. For example, the Maryland "Save our Streams" program — one of the earliest in the U.S. — began a conservation initiative in 1969 which expanded nationally in 1974. In all cases, utilizing volunteers to identify, capture, tag, and categorize observations and data allows all of these groups to enlarge the scope of their study, giving them better, more reliable results.

C-science involves ordinary people in large-scale data collection and analysis, usually to study some aspect of the natural world, and often under the project leadership of a professional scientist or scholar. While projects in environmental science, astronomy, and bird migration are popular, there are thousands of active investigations in all areas of science. Scientists benefit from having data collected by hundreds or thousands of volunteers and students, while the volunteers gain experience and personal pleasure collecting, observing and helping to analyze data in scientifically designed projects.

C-science is sometimes conflated with service learning, since both involve student volunteers for a "real" purpose. However C-science projects are unique in that scientists or experts manage the research design and analysis, but employ large numbers of volunteers to conduct very specific observations, measurements, or tests. Sometimes data collection happens "in the field" and sometimes it is done via computer, for example marking up medical scans or looking for numbers branded onto sea lions. These options mean that citizen science is not merely for those with the means to take students on field trips: all students can be engaged without leaving the building.

Finding a right-fit project

Finding the right project may seem like a bit of a chicken and egg problem. Unless you want to design your own study — and portals like http://zooniverse.org/lab have protocols for how to do this — most of us will be searching lists of projects to find those that align with a topic or standard. Thorough vetting of the project on the front end will help you design the best experience for you and your students. Some engage participants in the design and are focused on collecting data that can withstand peer review; others are preliminary experiments used as proof of concept. Understanding who funds and manages the research is important in order to decipher the agendas or desired outcomes of the project.

Here are some questions to consider as you begin looking for a citizen science project:

» How much training of volunteers is offered?

» Has this project (or, if using an online portal like SciStarter.com or Zooniverse.org) worked with high school students before?

» Are there videos, online tutorials, and other teaching resources available?

» What is the role of the lead scientists? Do they have an outreach or instructional team member who is available for questions or assistance? Are the scientists teaching allies and in communication with participants directly, or do they direct the research behind the scenes?

» Can you discern political or social perspectives, and are you comfortable discussing these?

» Is there an obvious educational goal, or are objectives primarily related to "doing science" or service learning work?

» How social is the team with its citizen scientists? Some online projects use Twitter, email newsletters, tagging within online platforms, and even gamified features like leaderboards to keep volunteers engaged. Are their communications and platforms compatible with your school's policies?

» How participatory is the project design? Could you and your students have input in methods and instruments?

» How much redundancy is in place? In other words, if your students decide to mis-tag wildlife photos, are there enough other people looking at the same photo that the "joke" will be ignored? In most cases, there is far more redundancy in online projects than you might anticipate. For example, the Michigan Zoomin project (https://www.zooniverse.org/projects/michiganzoomin/michigan-zoom-in), which seeks to gather baseline data about Michigan wildlife in various locations around the state, serves up each of its hundreds of thousands of images to *fifteen* participants. Even if your class clown thinks she's just sabotaged the research, she hasn't.

Defining success

Considering your teaching objectives, how you will define success? Are you interested in having students contribute to solving a scientific problem in your community? Seeing students read more science news? Having students gain fluency in working with large datasets? Encouraging students to view science as a form of civic engagement? Or maybe success is that your students become "hooked" on C-science and seek to contribute to another C-science project.

Scope

Do you want this project to have local or national impact? For example, those participating in Cornell's eBird project contribute their own local birdwatching data to a national dataset that has benefits far beyond their local community, whereas those who count turtles at a local beach will have greater grassroots impact. A decision about scope will determine the scale, number of volunteers, and size of the data set. Another variation on this question is to ask: Will the data only flow one way — from your students to the project — or do the scientists provide feedback and disseminate results back to your students?

Topic

Think about your curricular objectives. For example, what area of curriculum interests you and your students, enhances their passion for science, or supports scientific principles like classification or discovery? Whenever possible, involve your high school students in the process of matching selection criteria to a project! Browsing sites like SciStarter (https://scistarter.com/page/Educators.html) or Zooniverse.org can show students the breadth and depth of potential projects and create great classroom discussions. California Academy of Sciences shares tips for guiding students through the choice (https://www.calacademy.org/educators/lesson-plans/choose-your-own-citizen-science-project#search).

Feeling more ambitious? The Cornell Lab of Ornithology has an excellent toolkit (http://www.birds.cornell.edu/citscitoolkit/toolkit/toolkit) for designing your own project in any scientific area and offers advice on everything from question formulation to finding volunteers and collecting, analyzing, and disseminating data.

Type of engagement

What kind of *experience* do you want for your students – contributing to data collection or learning the process of experimentation? Delighting in photographs of animals in the wild or learning to prepare specimens for review? Doing field work or staying in front of a computer screen? Some goals might be to foster inquiry, enhance engagement, improve science process skills, or gain understanding of the nature of Big Data sets. If you want them to analyze data, what kinds of data literacy skills are required?

The type of engagement you choose will also dictate the amount of time spent on the project. Doing field work will require time away from the classroom (think multiple field trips) whereas identification of computer images can be done individually at home or as a whole-class activity at school.

Prior knowledge

What kind of *preparation* will your students need prior to engaging in a project? Perhaps, in order to participate in a citizen science project, they will need to know how to accurately measure liquids, count ladybug spots, take a water sample, or understand how cells replicate. They might also need practical advice, such as wearing (or avoiding) bug spray, perfume, or sunscreen. Without that context, students may be *active* without *actively learning*.

Timing

Consider, too, the season and *time of year*. Some citizen science projects require a burst of rapid-fire volunteer input and complete quickly. Others last over several months or years, with ongoing data collection, analysis, and new opportunities for input as the projects unfold. Does starting early in the year allow for a longer partnership with a C-science project? Are there certain projects — such as bird tracking — that can only be done in summer or early fall before birds migrate for the winter or deciduous trees drop their leaves? Are there certain seasons in which getting students out in nature or onscreen for a virtual project are a better fit for the academic year?

Some studies go on for years. If you want your students to get feedback on the data they've contributed, make sure the project's timeline will accommodate those needs. On the other hand, you may not want to be the first group to sign up; some suggest that the project should be in at least its second year of data collection.

Sources for projects

Now that you have brought your aspirations for C-science into focus, you're ready to find a project that match your learning goals. Some projects are already featured in the case studies in this section of the book. Here are some of our favorites.

Project portals

These sites can be a good start for schools because there are numerous projects on a single website. So with a single log-in and similar interfaces for each project, students can move quickly from one project to another.

Scistarter.com (https://scistarter.com/page/Educators.html) was updated and redesigned in 2017 and, as of press time, featured nearly 900 projects from which to choose! Projects at the time of publication include photographing clouds or overflowing water, documenting flu cases around you, contributing editing skills to a video about the 2017 eclipse, and air monitoring. You can help NASA, U.S. National Parks, weather networks, and the U.S. Geological Survey. You can browse from the home page or check out the Educator's page, which sorts projects by elementary, middle, or high school levels

Zooniverse.org has numerous wildlife projects as well as those in transcribing and digitizing historical papers and artifacts. As of press time, you could help the National Oceanic and Atmospheric Administration monitor Steller sea lions or identify cyclone patterns, lend University of Michigan researchers a hand in tracking Michigan wildlife, read and transcribe the diaries of British World War I soldiers for the Imperial War Institute and Britain's National Archives, or help scholars identify beach plastic from photos taken by drones.

Smithsonian Transcription (https://transcription.si.edu) lets you interact with documents and resources from its many museums. Many projects ask project "volunpeers" to retype or describe content that is photographed but not machine-readable. As of press time, projects included transcribing the notebooks of an Arctic explorer, a book explaining 18th century compound interest, the materials of Harvard's earliest female astronomers, or correspondence between global art dealers.

CitizenScience.gov (https://www.citizenscience.gov/) is the hub for citizen science and crowdsourced projects run by various government agencies. At the time this book went to press, projects included public health tracking for the Centers for Disease Control, the U.S. Army Corps's annual Midwinter Bald Eagle Survey, and the U.S. Immigrations and Customs Enforcement's app to try to catch child predators.

Finding aids

These sites list citizen science sites of interest:

Scientific American has a comprehensive lists of citizen science projects (https://www.scientificamerican.com/citizen-science/). While some projects point to Zooniverse or SciStarter already, others are standalone sites. Be sure to check project dates – some projects listed are no longer seeking volunteers. At press time, open projects include in-person habitat monitoring in the Florida Keys, an annual survey of trees in California and Oregon to monitor for Sudden Oak Death, and a University of Oklahoma soil collection project. For app-based citizen science, try the publication's list at https://www.scientificamerican.com/article/8-apps-that-turn-citizens-into-scientists/ .

Wikipedia lists several ongoing and completed citizen science projects. Their list included, at the time this book went to press, the Audubon Christmas Bird Count (a tradition for over a century), the Big Butterfly Count, and projects from the California Academy of Sciences.

Individual project sites

Want to keep students from wandering into other projects instead of working on the one you hope for? Consider a standalone project site like one of these:

GalaxyZoo.org, a sister site to Zooniverse.org, asks volunteers to help classify galaxies.

The **Cornell Lab of Ornithology**, one of citizen science's longest and most successful citizen science initiatives, has several projects from counting birds at your back yard feeder to the complex eBird project for counting and tracking birds. See http://www.birds.cornell.edu/page.aspx?pid=1664 .

Fold It (http://fold.it), the University of Washington's gamified project that uses human puzzle-solving skills to figure out how proteins fold. Unlocking the secrets of protein folding could help doctors figure out how to undo the ravages of some diseases like Alzheimer's.

The USA Phenology Network is a consortium of numerous university, government, and research labs that studies phenology, or nature's cycles — the timing of things such as bird migration, insect emergence, and fall leaf color change. The Network's team members study the effect of climate change on plants, animals, and landscapes. See https://www.usanpn.org .

Nova Labs (http://www.pbs.org/wgbh/nova/labs/about/), based around the award-winning PBS television series, is a unique take on citizen science because it teaches students the skills to use professional data to draw conclusions across a wide range of scientific topics. This portal was designed for educators and students to choose an active experiment where they can learn to "think like scientists."

Don't see what you're looking for? We recommend this online search strategy: ["citizen science" AND a topic area AND a locale]. Note that the brackets represent the search box itself and should not be typed into the search engine!

Conclusion

Armed with a more nuanced understanding of citizen science and related projects in the humanities, educators can select a project that best matches curricular objectives and our students' abilities and interests. Knowing what you're looking for, you'll be delighted by how many citizen science projects are available to you and how many scientists are eager for your students' volunteer support.

BIG DATA

1. Unroll.me email tracking and data sale 172
2. Big Data and discrimination 176
3. Television sets collecting data without notifying consumers 180
4. Big Data and self-driving trucks 184
5. Predictive policing: The seduction of technology 188
6. Big Data in banking and loans 192
7. Bias in student predictive analytics data: Does it help or hinder
   potential prospects/relationships? 195
8. Cross conversion tracking: Linking in-store purchases with online ads 199
9. The ethics of Mechanical Turk 204
10. The dark side of data: Using data as a means of stalking, surveilling, or
    preying on vulnerable populations 208

1. Unroll.me email tracking and data sale

Tyler Hoff

Do you get too much email but don't want to miss announcements of your favorite stores' sales? Do you wish your email system could sense all of your not-quite-junk but not-quite-useless email and put it all in one place for when you were ready to read it? That service is exactly what Unroll.me, owned by Slice Intelligence, said it would do — filter, organize, and remove your email subscriptions and present them to you in a single email, reducing email clutter. It sounded like a game-changer.

Then, in the *New York Times*' April 2017 piece on ride-sharing service Uber and its founder, Travis Kalanick, there was a brief mention of Uber's efforts to gather intelligence on its competitors. The *Times* made mention of one of those efforts: buying anonymized receipts issued by Uber competitor Lyft that had been harvested from emails accessed by the service Unroll.me. Unroll.me promised to help users organize and remove subscriptions from their email inboxes. As it turned out, a clause buried in the terms of service all users agreed to allowed Slice to sell their data as it saw fit.

This case study explores the tensions that can be surfaced when a company engages in large-scale data collection behind the scenes while marketing itself as a customer-facing solution.

Resources

Biddle, Sam. 2017. "Stop Using Unroll.me, Right Now. It Sold Your Data to Uber. *Intercept*, April 24. Accessed July 30, 2017. https://

theintercept.com/2017/04/24/stop-using-unroll-me-right-now-it-sold-your-data-to-uber/ .

Dawson, Jan. 2017. "The Uproar Over Unroll.me Selling User Data to Uber Shows Most People Don't Understand Ad-based Business Models." *Recode*, April 28. Accessed July 30, 2017. https://www.recode.net/2017/4/28/15454018/unroll-me-controversy-data-uber-ad-based-business-models-free-service .

Ghosh, Shona. 2017. "People are Freaking Out Because Email Decluttering Service Unroll.me Sold Their Data to Uber." *Business Insider*, April 24. Accessed July 30, 2017. http://www.businessinsider.com/people-are-freaked-out-that-unrollme-sold-email-data-to-uber-2017-4 .

Isaac, Mike and Steve Lohr. 2017. "Unroll.me Service Faces Backlash Over a Widespread Practice: Selling User Data." *New York Times*, April 24. Accessed July 30, 2017. https://www.nytimes.com/2017/04/24/technology/personal-data-firm-slice-unroll-me-backlash-uber.html .

Klosowski, Thorin. 2017. "Unroll.me, the Email Unsubscription Service, Has Been Collecting and Selling Your Data." *Lifehacker*, April 24. Accessed July 30, 2017. https://lifehacker.com/unroll-me-the-email-unsubscription-service-has-been-c-1794593445 .

Wu, Frank. 2017. "Why I Still Use Unroll.me — and What's Wrong With That." *Huffington Post*, May 8. Accessed July 30, 2017. http://www.huffingtonpost.com/entry/why-i-still-use-unrollme-and-whats-wrong-with_us_591092a6e4b056aa2363d765 .

Discussion questions

1. What are the key issues and perspectives in this case?

2. The Internet Archive has a long-standing project – called the Wayback Machine – to archive web pages over time. Go to http://web.archive.org and type unroll.me into the search bar. Find the version of the site archived before the *New York Times* story broke on April 24, 2017. Compare that home page to the current one. What is the same, and what is different? What language do you see about the benefits and risks of using the tool? Was Unroll.me's marketing appropriately descriptive of the service? Explain your response.

3. Permission to harvest data from emails *was* in the end user license agreement (EULA) that subscribers agreed to when they registered for Slice's free Unroll.me service. Is what Slice/Unroll.me did OK? Why or why not?

4. Did Slice/Unroll.me have an obligation to compensate for the fact that most people either skip reading EULAs or are sidelined by EULAs' length or legal language? Do you think consumers should actively take measures to prevent their data from being sold in this manner?

5. Do you think the large public outcry against Unroll.me was warranted? Why or why not?

6. Several of the articles above state some version of, "If you're not paying for it, you're the product," meaning that you are "paying" for so-called free services by contributing your data and personal information. Do you think this is always true? If so, how much more thought do you think consumers should put into which services they use?

7. Is it practical for users to avoid all services that might try to sell their data in this way? Explain your thinking.

8. Google recently announced that Gmail would stop harvesting user data from emails sent and received, a practice it had engaged in since Gmail's public release in order to customize ads served up to individual accountholders. Was what Slice Intelligence did substantially different from what Google was doing? Why or why not?

9. Google has stopped Gmail from operating in this way, but all other Google services harvest user data for sale in some way. Should consumers stop using Google services? As a follow-up, if consumers did stop using Google services in large numbers, what would the consequences be?

10. How can users work to be more aware of what services are doing with their data? Some argue that the simple answer to scenarios like these is to just always read the terms of service agreement. Is this a reasonable expectation? Why or why not?

2. Big Data and discrimination

Jo Angela Oehrli

Big Data seems to be invading our lives. From how it influences our car insurance premiums to the kinds of information we see online, Big Data is pervasive. Big Data is not just everywhere though. It's constantly behind the scenes making decisions and drawing conclusions for us. And while it's great, for example, that banks can notice when your banking behavior changes, it can be disturbing to consider that banks know where you are based on your purchases. It can be even more disturbing to realize that software and algorithms are making decisions about you without the benefit of human intervention.

The use of Big Data can be both a benefit and a hindrance because it illuminates our actions and cultures in many ways and then it tries to digitize future thinking. For example, politicians can point to data about the United States prison population as evidence of the high rate of incarceration of the African American male population. The conclusions we draw about those high rates of incarceration may provide evidence of past discriminatory practices. Or consider this: what if judges decided what a convicted criminal's sentence would be based predictions of *future*, not past, crimes? Algorithms like that might have been designed to protect society, but should a current crime's punishment be based on the *possibility* of future criminality without human intervention? An unintended consequence could be that the cycle of discrimination would continue.

Americans seem to inherently value equality and have huge faith in how technology can level any playing field. Against that backdrop, the question of whether technology could potentially perpetuate inequality is an urgent one. In this case study, we'll consider how Big Data has the potential to both help us address current discriminatory practices and perpetuate past inequalities.

Resources

Brogan, Jacob. 2016. "FTC Report Details How Big Data Can Discriminate Against the Poor." *Future Tense*, January 7. Accessed July 27, 2017. http://www.slate.com/blogs/future_tense/2016/01/07/ftc_report_shows_big_data_can_discriminate_against_the_poor.html .

Executive Office of the President. 2016. "Big Data: A Report on Algorithmic Systems, Opportunity, and Civil Rights." May. Accessed July 27, 2017. https://obamawhitehouse.archives.gov/sites/default/files/microsites/ostp/2016_0504_data_discrimination.pdf .

Federal Trade Commission. 2016. "Big Data: A Tool for Inclusion or Exclusion?" *FTC Report*, January. Accessed July 27, 2017. https://www.ftc.gov/system/files/documents/reports/big-data-tool-inclusion-or-exclusion-understanding-issues/160106big-data-rpt.pdf .

Noyes, Katherine. 2015. "Will Big Data Help End Discrimination—or Make It Worse?" *Fortune*, January 15. Accessed July 27, 2017. http://fortune.com/2015/01/15/will-big-data-help-end-discrimination-or-make-it-worse/ .

Schrage, Michael. 2014. "Big Data's Dangerous New Era of Discrimination." *Harvard Business Review*, January 29. Accessed July 27, 2017. https://hbr.org/2014/01/big-datas-dangerous-new-era-of-discrimination .

Sigdyal, Pradip. 2016. "Critics Allege Big Data Can Be Discriminatory, but Is It Really Bias?" *CNBC*, May 8. Accessed July 27, 2017. http://www.cnbc.com/2016/05/07/critics-allege-big-data-can-be-discriminatory-but-is-it-really-bias.html .

Timm, Alex. 2017. "Big Data Can Solve Discrimination." *Insurance Thought Leadership*, April 4. Accessed July 27, 2017.

http://insurancethoughtleadership.com/big-data-can-solve-discrimination/ .

United States Census Bureau, United States Department of Urban Development, United States Department of Commerce. 2016. "The Opportunity Project." Accessed July 27, 2017. https://opportunity.census.gov/ .

United States Equal Employment Opportunity Commission. 2016. "Use of Big Data Has Implications for Equal Employment Opportunity, Panel Tells EEOC." October 13. Accessed July 27, 2017. https://www.eeoc.gov/eeoc/newsroom/release/10-13-16.cfm .

Discussion questions

1. How is Big Data improving our lives now? What is the potential for improvement in the future?

2. What are some examples of how Big Data has been used to discriminate? Do you see the discrimination as intentional or as an accidental byproduct of well-intentioned people? Why do you see it that way? If it is accidental, how can well-intentioned people address the issue?

3. Who is likely to benefit from the use of Big Data? How does the identity of those beneficiaries inform issues around discrimination?

4. Based on the readings, who has been most affected by discrimination in Big Data? Why do you think those populations are disproportionately impacted?

5. Can you think of other examples when the advance of technology has had intended or unintended negative con-

sequences? What can we learn from those examples when considering Big Data and discrimination today?

6. From where does the Opportunity Project get its data? How has it helped to harness Big Data for positive impact? From what you see, what is the project doing to ensure that the data is not being used in a discriminatory fashion?

7. After reading the Timm piece, browse a few other articles on the *Insurance Thought Leadership* website. What, if any, interests does the insurance industry have that might influence their thoughts on discrimination and the use of Big Data? Do you see other authors on this list whose perspective might be less objective? Why?

8. Regardless of intent, how do we work toward minimizing Big Data's potential for discrimination today?

9. Do you think that Big Data will likely lead to discrimination in the future? Why or why not?

3. Television sets collecting data without notifying consumers

Jole Seroff

Beginning in 2014, Vizio manufactured internet-enabled televisions that continuously tracked and retrieved records of what consumers watched through proprietary software which was turned on by default. Vizio earned revenue by selling data about consumers' television viewing history to third parties for three uses:

1. audience measurement;
2. analyzing advertising effectiveness (in such cases data was used "in the aggregate"); and
3. targeting advertising to particular consumers on their other digital devices based on their television viewing habits.

No names were attached to the data sold to third parties; however, it did include details such as sex, age, income, education, and marital status. Along with these details, Vizio provided their clients highly-specific, second-by-second information about television viewing activities in each household.

In February 2014, a remote update installed tracking software to older model Vizio TVs. After the update, a pop-up notification appeared onscreen for one minute, stating that Smart Interactivity had been enabled and directing consumers to the Vizio website for more information. This notification provided no information about the collection or transmission of viewing data.

Ultimately, the Federal Trade Commission fined Vizio $2.2 million for the unauthorized collection of this data, and Vizio was required to delete all of the data it collected under this program.

Resources

Angwin, Julia. 2015. "Own a Vizio Smart TV? It's Watching You." *ProPublica*, November 9. Accessed June 6, 2017. https://www.propublica.org/article/*own-a-vizio-smart-tv-its-watching-you* .

Federal Trade Commision. 2017. *Christopher S. Porrino v. Vizio, Inc.2:17-cv-00758*, Feburary 6. Accessed October 28, 2017. https://www.ftc.gov/system/files/documents/cases/170206_vizio_2017.02.06_complaint.pdf . (pages 4 - 11 have the key information)

"How to turn on or off Video ACR/Viewing Data Collection (also known as ' Smart Interactivity')". 2017. Vizio. Accessed October 28, 2017. https://www.vizio.com/viewingdata . (Current Vizio website on how to change privacy settings)

Maheshwari, Sapna. 2017. "Is Your Vizio Television Spying on You? What to Know." *New York Times*, February 7. Accessed June 6, 2017. https://www.nytimes.com/2017/02/07/business/vizio-television-vizio-collected-viewers-habits-consent.html .

Discussion questions

1. Some of the data about consumers that Vizio collected and sold was aggregated, showing trends in groups, while some was associated with individual users. In your opinion, is there a significant difference between these two ways of packaging consumer data for sale to third parties?

2. How much specific information about an individual consumer would constitute a violation of privacy?

3. Some invasions of privacy are egregious, like knowing that a hacker has posted your username and password online or discovering that someone has engaged in identity theft with your identity. In this case, the company would know when you watched television and what you watched. To what degree are you comfortable with this information being siphoned out of your television, potentially without your knowledge? Is TV viewing data worthy of protection? What kinds of conclusions, including possibly erroneous ones, could others draw about you based on TV data?

4. Owners of Vizio TVs always had the option to go into their settings and turn off the software that was collecting their viewing data. Is the opportunity to opt out sufficient? Or should the law require that consumers opt in, effectively requiring default settings to prioritize consumer privacy?

5. What kinds of anonymized data should companies be empowered to collect for the purpose of improving their product? What about for the purpose of building new profit areas by selling this data?

6. Consumers' viewing history is covered under certain privacy protections. As we see in the FTC filings linked above, "Practices are not permitted if they are likely to cause harm to consumers and that is *not outweighed by countervailing benefits to consumers or competition*" (see page 174). Do you believe there is potential injury to consumers in the gathering and selling of this data? What do you think would be the potential benefits to consumers or competition?

7. The law also protects consumers from misrepresentations or deceptive omission of relevant information. Would you argue that setting the televisions to record and transmit

details of viewing behavior by default constitutes intentional concealment? Or is it the consumer's responsibility to discover what information her electronics are recording and transmitting about her behaviors? How would you define the consumer's responsibilities with regards to protecting her own privacy?

8. Vizio television sets tend to be priced at a lower price point than other television brands. Could you argue that Vizio's practices were beneficial or harmful to consumers with lower incomes?

9. Other electronics companies also collect this sort of data about customers, but only after customers have opted into the program. Further, other companies don't seem to have sold data that can be used to link that viewing data to other devices a consumer owns. In Vizio's business model, the data about a consumer's viewing habits were associated with an IP address; because the IP address is linked to any internet-connected devices in the home, Vizio's sale of this data enabled advertisers target ads to a consumer's other devices, such as a phone or tablet, based on what she had watched on television. When the data about TV viewing habits is used to reach the same consumers in other venues, does this constitute an important distinction with regard to privacy?

4. Big Data and self-driving trucks

Debbie Abilock

Long-haul automated trucking is being tested by multiple companies aiming for benefits in productivity, health, and safety. Like self-driving cars, autonomous trucks (with back-up professional drivers) are equipped with sensors, lasers, video cameras, and guidance systems which gather and process massive amounts of data.

The goal of Daimler, Otto, Peterbilt, Volvo, and other companies is to use this data to enable four-ton (80,000-pound) behemoths to steer, accelerate, and brake as skillfully as experienced professional truckers do under challenging road conditions, in problematic weather, and surrounded by vehicles driven by less predictable human drivers.

Recent events have raised questions of privacy and cybersecurity for all self-driving vehicles. The benefits of continual operation at optimal speed and the mitigation of errors made by sleep-deprived truckers are counterweighted by the special concerns of long-haul driving such as the maneuverability and stability of massive vehicles; regular transportation of hazardous cargos; and the potential loss of blue-collar jobs.

The costs of testing self-driving trucks are much higher than for self-driving cars, so extensive highway trials of heavy vehicles has yet to occur. This interval offers us opportunities for thoughtful policies and regulations in advance of a general roll-out of long-haul trucking with varying levels of driver automation.

Autonomous trucking has additional complexities beyond those for personal autonomous vehicles given its unique economic pressures: salaried drivers and businesses' expectations of rapid delivery. The constellation of articles presented below provide a broad landscape of the issues related to the trucking industry, including

- safe working conditions for drivers;
- potential impact on commerce and employment;
- industry definitions of levels of autonomy;
- planning for effective testing of autonomous or semi-autonomous trucks; and
- permitted activities on a state-by-state level.

If time allows, we encourage your participants to read most or all of these articles. If time is limited, consider asking participants to divide into small groups, each taking one or two articles, and then summarizing the key information for the larger group.

Resources

Bukszpan, Daniel. 2016. "Could Autonomous Trucks be the Next Weapon for Terrorists?" *CNBC*, July 21. Accessed July 7, 2017. http://www.cnbc.com/2016/07/21/could-autonomous-trucks-be-the-next-weapon-for-terrorists.html .

Ford, Martin. 2017. "Driverless Trucks: Economic Tsunami May Swallow One of Most Common US Jobs." *The Guardian*, February 16. Accessed July 7, 2017. https://www.theguardian.com/technology/2017/feb/16/self-driving-trucks-automation-jobs-trucking-industry .

International Brotherhood of Teamsters. 2017. "Putting the Brakes on Platooning: UPS Teamsters Raise Concerns on Connected Vehicle Technology." *Teamsters*, March 30. Accessed July 7, 2017. https://teamster.org/news/2017/03/putting-brakes-platooning-ups-teamsters-raise-concerns-connected-vehicle-technology .

Ockedahl, Carina. 2016. "The U.S. Trucking Industry's Top 10 Issues." *Trucks.com*, November 26. Accessed July 7, 2017. https://www.trucks.com/2015/11/26/us-trucking-industrys-top-10-issues/.

Ryvola, Scott. n.d. "Otto - Testing Operations: Daily Road Tests." *Consumer Watchdog*. Accessed April 23, 2017.. http://www.consumerwatchdog.org/sites/default/files/resources/otto_testing_operations2.pdf.

Semuels, Alana. 2017. "When Robots Take Bad Jobs." *Atlantic*, February 27. Accessed July 7, 2017. https://www.theatlantic.com/business/archive/2017/02/when-robots-take-bad-jobs/517953/.

Simpson, John M. 2017. John M. Simpson Letter to Jean Shiomoto, "Complaint regarding Otto's Testing of Self-driving Trucks and Uber's Robot Cars," February 7. *Consumer Watchdog*. Accessed July 7, 2017. http://www.consumerwatchdog.org/sites/default/files/resources/ltrdmv020717.pdf.

Society of Automotive Engineers. 2014. "Automated Driving: Levels of Driving Automation Are Defined in New SAE International Standard J3016." *SAE International*. Accessed July 7, 2017. https://www.sae.org/misc/pdfs/automated_driving.pdf.

Weiner, Gabriel, and Bryant Walker Smith. 2012. "Automated Driving: Legislative and Regulatory Action." CIS, February 12. Accessed July 7, 2017. http://cyberlaw.stanford.edu/wiki/index.php/Automated_Driving:_Legislative_and_Regulatory_Action.

Wright, Matthew. 2017. "What Will Driverless Trucks Mean for Highway Safety?" Wright Law PLC Blog, January 16. Accessed July 7, 2017. https://www.truckinjurylaw.us/blog/what-will-driverless-trucks-mean-for-highway-safety/.

Discussion questions

1. How are the challenges of developing self-driving trucks different from those for self-driving cars?

2. What do major stakeholders – truckers, trucking companies, and government – agree are the most important issues to be resolved?

3. Brainstorm how each of these issues could be addressed via incentives, voluntary policies, government regulation, and legislation.

4. Which combination of ideas in Question 3 offers the most promising benefits in comprehensively addressing stakeholder concerns?

5. If you prioritize these possible solutions, how would you order them from high to low?

6. What criteria did you use to rank them? Why? Whose perspectives are most satisfied in your priorities?

7. What stakeholder concerns are poorly represented? How might these be addressed by modifying your solutions?

8. Does anything you have discussed in this case study change how you feel about self-driving personal vehicles? Why or why not?

5. Predictive policing: The seduction of technology

Susan Smith

The 2002 sci-fi film *Minority Report* describes a future where policing is guided by troves of data that will predict where and by whom crimes will be committed. There are indications that predictive policing — using past data to predict where future crimes may occur — is gaining widespread acceptance today in some of the nation's largest cities.

Algorithms have been developed to use Big Data to help police focus on locations and people most likely to be associated with crime. While these tools are intended to reduce bias and racial profiling, they may instead reinforce and amplify the prejudices they seek to eliminate.

While predictive policing could potentially be used to study officer behavior or help with mental health interventions, to date most initiatives serve to validate and reinforce unfair law enforcement practices, especially among people of color.

Debate over how we reconcile civil rights law with the collection of this data, who should have access to the data, and the profit motives of the corporations that sell body cameras and cloud storage that collect and store the data are very real concerns.

Resources:

Hatmaker, Tyler. 2017. "With AI Investments, Taser Could Use Its Body Camera Division for Predictive Policing." *TechCrunch*, April 30. Accessed June 9, 2017. https://techcrunch.com/2017/04/30/taser-law-enforcement-technology-report/ .

Hvistendahl, Mara. 2016. "Can 'Predictive Policing' Prevent Crime Before it Happens?" *Science Magazine*, September 28. Accessed June 6, 2017. http://www.sciencemag.org/news/2016/09/can-predictive-policing-prevent-crime-it-happens .

Kavanaugh, Shane Dixon. 2017. "This Teen's Story is Your Worst 'Predictive Policing' Nightmare." *Vocativ*, April 12. Accessed June 6, 2017. http://www.vocativ.com/418541/predictive-policing-nightmare/ .

Kofman, Ava. 2017. "Taser Will Use Police Body Camera Videos 'To Anticipate Criminal Activity.'" *Intercept*, April 30. Accessed June 6, 2017. https://theintercept.com/2017/04/30/taser-will-use-police-body-camera-videos-to-anticipate-criminal-activity/ .

"Predictive Policing." 2014. National Institute of Justice, June 9. Accessed November 1, 2017. https://www.nij.gov/topics/law-enforcement/strategies/predictive-policing/Pages/welcome.aspx .

Smith, Jack IV. 2017. "An App that Pinpoints White-Collar Criminals Works like Predictive-Policing Software." *Business Insider*, April 25. Accessed June 6, 2017. http://www.businessinsider.com/this-app-shows-you-white-collar-criminals-2017-4 .

"Statement of Concern About Predictive Policing by ACLU and 16 Civil Rights Privacy, Racial Justice, and Technology Organizations." 2016. *American Civil Liberties Union*. August 31. Accessed November 1, 2017 https://www.aclu.org/other/statement-concern-about-predictive-policing-aclu-and-16-civil-rights-privacy-racial-justice .

Stroud, Matt. 2014. "The Minority Report: Chicago's New Police Computer Predicts Crimes, but is it Racist?" *Verge*, February 19. Accessed June 6, 2017. https://www.theverge.com/2014/2/19/5419854/the-minority-report-this-computer-predicts-crime-but-is-it-racist .

Discussion questions

1. Which civic and industry groups benefit most from the use of predictive policing as a strategy and a tool?

2. Can predictive policing be salvaged as a way to reduce crime? How could it be improved?

3. How do we reconcile the 4th Amendment right to prove "reasonable suspicion" as a condition of arrest with computer-generated probabilities based on location or social networks? Will the laws have to change to accommodate technology?

4. How might local governments be incentivized to invest in predictive tools for use beyond criminal behavior, to instead distribute social services or combat police brutality?

5. What businesses or industries might be accidentally impacted by predictive policing? For example, how might predictive policing indicate "less safe" areas that might discourage tourism or restaurant visits in an area? How might real estate values be impacted?

6. With such tight security around the data these programs produce, who will audit the results and methodologies? Who should have access to the data?

7. Are you personally more comfortable with geospatial predictions of crime than with identification of potential criminals? Why might that be? Are there any pitfalls in thinking that *place* is a better indicator than *person*?

8. What are the pros and cons of using "deep learning" and AI when identifying patterns in policing practices from body cameras?

9. Discuss the potential privacy concerns with developing a "heat map" of a city's most dangerous people based on Big Data predictions. If, as described in the *Verge* article, these lists are not available under the Freedom of Information Act, as other civic documents are, what civil rights does a "potential" offender have?

10. Is free speech violated if social network posts are added to the data used to identify the "most dangerous" people? Do these rights extend to online "speech?"

11. Does the expansion of predictive policing into white collar crime equal the playing field or extend self-reinforcing crime fighting into yet a new area?

6. Big Data in banking and loans

Kelly Hovinga

Big data is the collection of personal data, such as browsing history, address, age, gender, and purchasing habits. Personal data can be collected by companies who specialize in gathering information, or it can be done by companies like Facebook and Google, but the uses are largely the same. Companies rely on Big Data brokers to create user profiles, which are often used for marketing. A home insurance company will be interested in targeting people who have just bought homes. A car company that sells minivans will be interested in targeting families with more than one child. The collection of personal profiles allow companies to target particular segments of a population for the products and services they offer.

Use of Big Data has increased at an exponential rate over the last few years, and with its growth, so has its applications. In the United States, there are actually no laws that specifically prohibit the use of Big Data. Instead, companies regulate their Big Data usage by comparing their proposed project with privacy policies, contractual agreements, and laws related to consumer discrimination.

In the banking industry, the two major limiting factors in the usage of Big Data are the Fair Credit Reporting Act and the Equal Credit Opportunity Act. Despite these regulations, there are concerns that Big Data is being used to discriminate against different groups in the case of loan applications, mortgages, and other bank related services.

In this case study, you'll look at how Big Data is being used in marketing and banking — with sometimes unanticipated results.

Resources

Chintamaneni, Prasad. 2016. "How Banks are Capitalizing on a New Wave of Big Data and Analytics." *Harvard Business Review*, November 22. Accessed June 11, 2017. https://hbr.org/sponsored/2016/11/how-banks-are-capitalizing-on-a-new-wave-of-big-data-and-analytics .

Higgins, John K. 2016. "FTC Issues Regulatory Warning on Big Data Use." *Commerce Times*, January 20. Accessed June 6, 2017. http://www.ecommercetimes.com/story/83004.html .

Noyes, Katherine. 2015. "Will Big Data Help End Discrimination— or Make it Worse?" *Fortune*, January 15. Accessed June 11, 2017. http://fortune.com/2015/01/15/will-big-data-help-end-discrimination-or-make-it-worse/ .

Ramirez, Edith and Julie Brill, Maureen Ohlhausen, and Terrell McSweeny. 2016. "Big Data: A Tool for Inclusion or Exclusion?" *Federal Trade Commission*, January. Accessed June 9, 2017. https://www.ftc.gov/system/files/documents/reports/big-data-tool-inclusion-or-exclusion-understanding-issues/160106big-data-rpt.pdf .

Sicklick, Jeremy. 2017. "How Will Big Data Transform the Mortgage Lending Industry?" *MReport*, February 6. Accessed June 11, 2017. http://www.themreport.com/news/02-06-2017/will-big-data-transform-mortgage-lending-industry .

Discussion questions

1. What details about your life produce a digital footprint? What in your life would you prefer that banks and mortgage lenders not know about you?

2. What is a *proxy* and how can it be used? What are some of the limitations to using a proxy for predictive algorithms?

3. Why would banks find the use of Big Data helpful?

4. A number of companies have written algorithms that significantly reduce the likelihood of credit fraud, and thus pre-emptively save banks money. However, what are some issues with determining the risk of an applicant by Big Data profiles and algorithms?

5. What is the position the FTC report takes on the use of Big Data in targeting groups and assessing risks? Do you agree with it? What might they have overlooked? Underemphasized? Why should businesses have access to Big Data?

6. What are some of the laws in place to protect users? Do you think they are enough? Why or why not?

7. How do the perspectives of the resource authors affect their message? What are some of the limitations on the various views?

8. Considering the article from *MReport*, do you think businesses are listening to the ethical position in the FTC report? How did you decide your answer?

9. What is the ethical difference between using personal data to target people for ads and using personal data to rush people through mortgage approvals?

7. Bias in student predictive analytics data: Does it help or hinder potential prospects/relationships?

Susan D. Ballard

Predictive analytics is the practice of employing various statistical methods to examine current and historical information to forecast what may transpire in a particular area or in relation to a particular behavior in the future. It is increasingly used in education to assist teachers and administrators in their assessments of what interventions or programs will help students to achieve higher rates of success or mastery of content. That sounds like progress and a real help to schools where needs are high but budgets for interventions are limited.

However, student panel participants at the EduCon 2.9 conference expressed concern. A student at Macomb Community College in Michigan said, "We don't know who is choosing [the data] and who is pulling the strings." In summarizing that conference session, Dobo (2017a) condensed their concern, saying that students "worry that the data will be used to label them before they have a chance to make their own impressions on a teacher."

Advocates of these predictive programs say they help educators find and help students at risk of failure, but the students on the panel presented another side of the story. What happens if this information is used against us? Will a digital dossier — possibly with inaccurate, incomplete or out-of-context data — follow us forever (Dobo 2017b)?

Resources

DeVaney, James. 2016. "How Can Learning Analytics Improve the Student Experience?" *EdSurge*, August 31. Accessed June 30, 2017. https://www.edsurge.com/news/2016-08-31-how-can-learning-analytics-improve-the-student-experience .

Dobo, Nichole. 2017a. "Students' Worry: Education Technology Might Predict Failure Before They Have a Chance to Succeed." *The Hechinger Report*, March 1. Accessed June 30, 2017. http://hechingerreport.org/students-worry-education-technology-might-predict-failure-chance-succeed/ .

Dobo, Nichole. 2017b. "When Using Data to Predict Outcomes, Consider the Ethical Dilemmas, New Report Urges: Researchers Say Colleges Need to Take Care In How They Use Predictive Analytics." *The Hechinger Report*, March 8. Accessed July 8 , 2017. http://hechingerreport.org/using-data-predict-outcomes-consider-ethical-dilemmas-new-report-urges/ .

Education Commission of the States. 2012. "Teacher Expectations of Students: A Self-fulfilling Prophecy?" *Progress of Education Reform* 13 (6). Accessed June 30, 2017. www.ecs.org/clearinghouse/01/05/51/10551.pdf .

Gomes, Amilcah. 2014. "Redefining 'At-risk' Through Predictive Analytics: A Targeted Approach to Enhancing Student Success." PowerPoint. Association of American Colleges and Universities. Chicago, IL. March 29. https://www.aacu.org/sites/default/files/files/meetings/dlss14_CS33.pdf .

Jackson, Abby. 2016. "College Admissions Teams are Ranking Students on a 0-10 Scale Based on Factors They Can't Control." *Business Insider*, October 27. Accessed June 30, 2017. http://www.businessinsider.com/the-perils-of-using-predictive-analytics-in-college-admissions-2016-10 .

Discussion questions

1. In the DeVaney article, how does the University of Michigan team frame predictive analytics as a positive? Which of their points feels most compelling? What concerns you?

2. In the DeVaney reading, the Michigan team asserts that predictive analytics can better personalize the learning experience. How might it do that? How might it not?

3. Consider the student voices in Dobo's "Students Worry" article (2017a). Could the use of predictive analytics, which is meant to accelerate student growth, restrict students options, choices, and futures? Can you envision any scenarios in which a student's past behavior might accurately or inaccurately predict future performance?

4. What if one of the data points fed into the system was a student's behavior record? Does that change how you feel about this issue?

5. Is it likely that "digital dossiers" will be used to help or hinder students in seeking education or career opportunities?

6. How do students who aren't good "test takers" deal with the reality of predictive analytics?

7. How will schools account for the fact that some of the instruments they rely on in predictive analytics (surveys, etc.) may have incorrect, misleading, or missing information?

8. The report by the Education Commission of the States indicates that teacher perceptions of student performance can

significantly impact actual performance, a phenomenon the report calls a "self-fulfilling prophecy." How might this phenomenon help some students? Hinder others? How might teacher preparation programs and/or colleges and universities intervene regarding potential student performance expectation bias by teachers?

9. Does what you now know about the data being collected and analyzed on the University of Michigan campus (primarily in large undergraduate courses, and only in a fraction of all courses) change your idea of what college will be like for future college students?

10. What can you do to ensure that your "dossier" portrays accurate information about you?

8. Cross conversion tracking: Linking in-store purchases with online ads

Kelly Hovinga

Monday you buy a pair of socks through Amazon. Then on Tuesday, you suddenly have six ads parading a variety of socks accross your computer screen as soon as you open your browsing window. The ability to track both browsing behavior and purchases is a trademark of the modern world. Google, Facebook, and Amazon are able to create personalized profiles of your online browsing and shopping habits down to what kind of items you buy online, how often you purchase them, when you purchase them, and how much you spend. Many companies now believe that the key to finding the perfect market is in big data algorithms, and thus a considerable amount of money can be found in online advertising. This case study will look at how the Big Data mentality transforms business practices in marketing.

Recently, Google unveiled a new campaign to track cross conversion purchases. Cross conversion tracking refers to a company's ability to track multi-device purchases, and thus create algorithms to predict purchasing habits. For example, an individual might be scrolling through scarves on her smartphone while waiting for the bus, and see something they really like in an ad – but not buy it. A week later, when she's on her laptop, she might go back to the store's website, or the store itself, and buy the scarf. Google is able to connect the smartphone behavior to the laptop activity when the individual is logged into their Google account on both devices. By buying credit card purchasing data from a source like Axciom, Google can now triangulate the data and know where purchases are being made at in-store locations (but only in terms of the store and total amount spent; they do not know the individual items purchased). By combining the two data sources, Google can often figure out whether your online browsing yielded a purchase at that store. The browsing/purchasing information is then anonymized and used as data to predict purchasing habits based off exposure to online advertising. Google's cross conversion tracking service is very useful to stores who want more precise data to better plan customer advertising campaigns. Google announced this campaign to companies that buy advertising from them in May of 2017. However, in July 2017, a privacy rights watchdog filed a legal complaint with the Federal Trade Commission.

The privacy watchdog wants the government to review Google's algorithm, wants the companies that sell Google the credit card information to be disclosed, and for opt out options for Google tracking to be more accessible and transparent. The opt out option for tracking is important, because if an individual is not signed into Google or is using Google's Incognito Mode, then behavior will not be attributed to that particular user; thus, that particular user will be untrackable. Similarly, if someone goes to a store but uses cash, that customer's identifying information (e.g., credit card number) cannot be tracked. In this case study, participants will become familiar with customer conversion tracking practices and discuss its relevance or lack of relevance to their lives as consumers.

Resources

Associated Press. 2017. "Google Starts Tracking Offline Shopping – What You Buy at Stores in Person." *Los Angeles Times*, May 23. Accessed June 30, 2017. http://www.latimes.com/business/technology/la-fi-tn-google-ads-tracking-20170523-story.html .

Dwoskin, Elizabeth, and Craig Timberg. 2017. "Google Now Knows When its Users Go to the Store and Buy Stuff."

Washington Post, May 23. Accessed June 30, 2017. https://www.washingtonpost.com/news/the-switch/wp/2017/05/23/google-now-knows-when-you-are-at-a-cash-register-and-how-much-you-are-spending/?utm_term=.5463b7398a9f .

Ramaswamy, Sirdhar. 2013. "Estimated Total Conversions: New Insight for the Multi-Screen World. *Google Inside AdWords*, October 1. Accessed June 30, 2017. https://adwords.googleblog.com/2013/10/estimated-total-conversions.html .

Taube, Aaron. 2014. "Google Will Now Track Your In-Store Purchases to Figure Out Whether Its Ads Are Effective." *Business Insider*, April 14. Accessed June 30, 2017. http://www.businessinsider.com/google-tracking-in-store-purchases-2014-4 .

Whitwam, Ryan. 2017. "Google Can Track Your Offline Purchases." *ET*, May 24. Accessed June 30, 2017. https://www.extremetech.com/internet/249770-google-can-now-track-offline-purchases .

Discussion questions

1. How would you explain cross conversion tracking to a neighbor? To someone who already advertises online? To a brick-and-mortar store in your community who is looking for ways to maximize revenue?

2. Why might Google have decided to create this technology in the first place? What might have motivated them to release this information in May 2017?

3. What might be some limitations in the analytics algorithms or linking online ads up with online purchases and in store purchases? Do you feel that your on- and offline shopping habits would be captured accurately? Why or why not?

4. Why might Google be unwilling to share the algorithms for creating the "double-blind" method of anonymizing data?

5. Some scholars have been able to take anonymized data and reconnect it to someone's identity. Does that change how you feel about the issue?

6. If the government — and not Google — were able to track your shopping behavior, would that change how you felt about the issue?

7. Tracking your in-store purchases doesn't just mean Google knows how much you spent at a store. It also means it is quite likely Google knows where you were at a particular time. Does that change how you feel about this issue?

8. Google is able to connect online and offline behavior because purchasing with a credit card creates a trail of data. Cash transactions cannot be tracked (unless, perhaps, one uses a customer loyalty card or customized coupon sometime in the future). Do these articles make you think differently about using cash versus a credit or debit card for your own family's purchases? Why or why not?

9. Sometimes, the same story can be reported in different ways in different publications. What is the general tone of the *Business Insider* article? The one from the *Washington Post*? What is the significance of the differences? Does either make you more or less confident about the issue? More or less comfortable?

10. If you had the power to change any ethical problems with this practice, what would you change it to? What kind of legislation would you like applied to the issue? Why?

11. Considering that individuals' personal spending and browsing data is already collected online, does linking that information up to in-store purchases make a considerable difference in personal privacy? Why or why not? Additionally, personal information comes from a large conglomeration of sources, making it difficult to determine where it came from. Do you think this influences Google's willingness to disclose their information providers?

12. Does reading about and discussing this issue make you want to take action of some kind, like changing your Google Privacy settings? Why or why not?

9. The ethics of Mechanical Turk

Wendy Steadman Stephens

The original Mechanical Turk (public domain).

Since 2005, Amazon has enabled access to a crowd labor exchange called Mechanical Turk (https://mturk.com), allowing anyone with Internet access to sign up to complete web-based microwork requiring human intelligence. Described as a "free market for digital labor," Mechanical Turk allows as-needed recruitment of individuals to perform tasks including transcribing handwritten forms, rating and tagging content, completing surveys, and writing captions. As independent contractors, those working as Mechanical Turkers are not bound by federal labor laws and consequently are frequently earning significantly less than the minimum wage.

The average wage for each task averages a few cents, and, if performed quickly, can generate around one dollar an hour in aggregate, before the 10 - 20% commission taken by Amazon and the self-employment taxes Turkers are required to pay on their earnings. Despite the absence of geographic barrier to participation, 80% of the people working as Turkers live in the United States.

Resources

Chaves, Zoe. 2014. "Amazon Mechanical Jerk." *Huffington Post*, January 23. Accessed May 30, 2017. http://www.huffingtonpost.com/zoe-chaves/amazon-mechanical-turk_b_4181977.html .

Chen, Michelle. 2016. "There's a Problem with 'Crowd Labor.'" *Nation*, July 29. Accessed May 30, 2017. https://www.thenation.com/article/mechanical-turk-gigifies-the-knowledge-economy/ .

Kessler, Sarah. 2015. "What Does a Union Look Like in the Gig Economy?" *Fast Company*, February 19. Accessed May 30, 2017. https://www.fastcompany.com/3042081/what-does-a-union-look-like-in-the-gig-economy .

Matias, J. Nathan. 2015. "The Tragedy of the Digital Commons." *Atlantic*, June 8. Accessed May 30, 2017. https://www.theatlantic.com/technology/archive/2015/06/the-tragedy-of-the-digital-commons/395129/ .

Matsakis, Louise. 2016. "Fifty Percent of Mechanical Turk Workers Have College Degrees, Study Finds." *Vice*, July 11. Accessed May 30, 2017. https://motherboard.vice.com/en_us/article/fifty-percent-of-mechanical-turk-workers-have-college-degrees-study-finds .

Wen, Shawn. 2014. "The Ladies Vanish." *New Inquiry*, November 11. Accessed May 30, 2017. https://thenewinquiry.com/the-ladies-vanish/ .

Discussion questions

1. Mechanical Turkers set their own hours and are not under any obligation to accept any particular task and can choose tasks that they find most interesting or the best paid. Why might this be attractive to potential workers? Is it attractive to you as a part-time supplemental job or as full-time freelance employment?

2. Mechanical Turk work requires available infrastructure in the form of computer access and connectivity. U.S. MTurkers have been found to be mostly female and white, and to be somewhat younger and more educated than the U.S. population overall. What are potential explanations for the demographic?

3. Requesters seeking to recruit Mechanical Turkers must provide a billing address in the U.S., Australia, Canada, or the UK. Some 80% of Mechanical Turk workers are located in the U.S. Does this seem to violate the spirit of federal labor regulations?

4. Approximately 30% of American workers are in the same category as MTurkers: independent contractors. Do you feel that is an accurate way to categorize gig economy opportunities like MTurkers, Uber drivers, and AirBnB hosts? Does it matter that five large companies post more than half of the tasks on the Mechanical Turk site?

5. Professors and researchers must "publish or perish," meaning that having new research about which to write academic articles is critical to how their career progress is evaluated. Today, there is greater competition for a shrinking pool of grant dollars. Some have found MTurk to be a cost-effective way to get a large quantity of survey data collected, images classified, or other feedback gathered. Might the platform's necessary emphasis on speed affect data quality?

6. Continuing on the research theme, discuss who the "average" MTurker is. If a researcher looks to this "average" user, will she get a representative sampling? What are the risks of MTurk as a survey or research population?

7. Translation is one of the tasks performed by Mechanical Turkers. Do you see this as a threat to professional translators? Why or why not?

8. The platform name is derived from a famous 18th century chess-playing automaton that appeared to play flawless chess or other board games. Nicknamed "the Turk," the mechanical mannequin stood behind a desk-like piece of furniture and appeared to make the moves himself. The Turk is said to have bested both Napoleon Bonaparte and Ben Franklin but was later revealed as a hoax when it was discovered that inside the cabinet, a human chess master was controlling the Turk. What does the name "Mechanical Turk" indicate about the platform's desire to obscure the human nature of the work in favor of the appearance of technical wizardry?

10. The dark side of data: Using data as a means of stalking, surveilling, or preying on vulnerable populations

Susan D. Ballard

Big Data, the umbrella term for harvesting numerous pieces of information about individuals and their personal preferences and collecting that information in huge repositories to be sorted by computer programs, has opened the door to the brokering or selling of that information to be used in various ways. Data can be collected about personal factors, interests, and lifestyle choices. That information comes from a variety of sources, and increasingly, those sources are being mashed together to yield even more precise profiles about who we are and what we do. Most of us are generating significant quantities of data via e-commerce, email, electronic health records, government data, and social media (including presence on particular sites, those with whom we have social connections, content and timing of social media posts, etc.) This has opened the door to the brokering or selling of that information to be used in various ways.

In many instances, this data can be used for our benefit, such as in the case of health care professionals sharing information in order to assure us of the best care. Conversely, the same data can be deliberately harvested to target specific individuals or groups in order to sell products, as well as to scam or scare people into taking action that may not be in their best interests.

In this case study, you'll explore how the increasing quantity of collected data can shift from being helpful to harmful, frightening, or manipulative and consider what best steps forward might be.

Resources

Crawford, Kate. 2014. "When Big Data Marketing Becomes Stalking." *Scientific American*, April 1. Retrieved June 16, 2017. https://www.scientificamerican.com/article/when-big-data-marketing-becomes-stalking1/ .

Crump, Catherine and Matthew Harwood. 2014. "Invasion of the Data Snatchers: Big Data and the Internet of Things Means the Surveillance of Everything." *American Civil Liberties Union*, March 25. Retrieved June 16, 2017. https://www.aclu.org/blog/speakeasy/invasion-data-snatchers-big-data-and-internet-things-means-surveillance-everything .

Gregg, Michael. 2016. "The Future of Digital Spying: Home Edition." *Huffington Post*, January 25. Retrieved June 16, 2017. http://www.huffingtonpost.com/michael-gregg/the-future-of-digital-spy_b_9068958.html .

Schneier, Bruce. 2017. "Data and Goliath: Four Ways You Can Protect Yourself from Digital Surveillance." *Huffington Post*. Retrieved June 16, 2017. http://www.huffingtonpost.com/bruce-schneier/data-and-goliath-digital-surveillance_b_6898162.html .

Wexler, Richard. 2016. "Big Data is Watching You: If Predictive Analytics Still Doesn't Creep You Out, Watch this Ad." *Chronicle of Social Change*, September 1. Retrieved June 16, 2017. https://chronicleofsocialchange.org/blogger-co-op/big-data-watching-predictive-analytics-still-doesnt-creep-watch-ad/20778 . (Note: While the link to the Ad referred to in this blog post is no longer active, the message still resonates.)

Discussion questions

1. Is there a need to establish norms for the responsible use of data? If so, who would administer and ensure compliance? Does your answer change depending on what type of organization might be managing your data (e.g., not-for-profit, government, corporation, school)?

2. Should companies and organizations be more transparent about their data collection? What can companies and organizations do to ensure their customers and clients understand and are willing to participate in the use of their personal data (beyond providing standard privacy policy statements which people tend to accept without reading)?

3. Is it important to ensure that both customers and clients understand the purpose of data capture and preservation as a means of having accurate information?

4. As people become more aware that companies/organizations are capturing and keeping data, should we be concerned that they will deliberately provide misleading or false information that may have negative impact? (See the Schneier post above).

5. How much say do you think you should have in who has access to and may broker data about you?

6. Some of the articles talk about dynamic pricing that adjusts depending on who the algorithms determine the customer is, using such indicators as zip code to determine income and level of education, etc. Do you think that is a fair practice for consumers? For businesses?

7. Opting out of some data collection can minimize what companies know about you, but it also might mean you lose eligibility for preferred pricing, coupons, or other discounts. How do you feel about that?

8. It's easier to opt out when you know that information is being captured. In some of these articles, customers' data (such as knowing a phone's location because it is pinging and looking for WiFi hotspots) is being captured without their knowledge. How do you feel about that?

ETHICAL DATA USE

1. The personal information you are giving away 214
2. Protecting student data in schools 217
3. SAT and ACT information: What happens to it? 220
4. Surveillance cameras in schools and the case of special education 223
5. Student privacy in the age of cloud storage 227
6. Big Data and government nudges 230
7. The fear factor: Hyped-up use of data to sway public opinion/behavior 234
8. Those smart devices are smarter than you think 237
9. Canaries in the mine: Chicago and Flint — haves vs. have-nots
   in use of data 240
10. The implications of privacy regulation on Internet privacy 243
11. Data philanthropy 247

1. The personal information you are giving away

Jennifer Colby

Which Disney Princess are you? What are your most-used words on Facebook? Which Hogwarts house would you be sorted into? Answering online quizzes is something many of us do everyday. But we freely give away personal information when we participate in these activities. Every click you make and every character you enter is monitored, analyzed, and sometimes shared with others.

Companies and marketers use this information about you to track your behavior in order to place ads that will sell you (and others) more products. They can also use your personal information to make connections with your online and offline self. Think about the personal information you may be giving away to entities you don't even know and what they might do with it.

Resources

Marshall, Jack. 2014. "Online Quizzes Are Data Goldmines for Marketers." *Wall Street Journal Blog*, September 14. Accessed May 30, 2017. http://blogs.wsj.com/cmo/2014/09/14/online-quizzes-are-data-goldmines-for-marketers/ .

Raphael, JR. 2009. "The Hidden Secrets of Online Quizzes." *PC World*, May 12. Accessed May 30, 2017. http://www.pcworld.com/article/164527/online_quizzes.html .

Wakefield, Jane. 2015. "Facebook Quizzes: What Happens to Your Data?" *BBC News*, November 26. Accessed May 30, 2017. http://www.bbc.com/news/technology-34922029 .

Discussion questions

1. What types of online quizzes have you answered? Make a list.

2. What are the benefits and drawbacks of answering online quizzes? Why do you answer online quizzes? Do you realize you are sharing personal information?

3. What types of personal information are you sharing when you answer online quizzes? How do you think a company might use that data in ways unrelated to the quiz? How do you feel about that?

4. Have you ever stopped answering a quiz while taking it? Why or why not?

5. What do you think about online ads? Do you pay attention to them? Have you ever bought something as a result of seeing an online ad? Why or why not? How do you feel when you've been browsing an online store and ads for what you just explored start popping up elsewhere?

6. What does it mean to "opt-in" or to "allow" a third-party entity to access your account?

7. According to *The Wall Street Journal* blog post above, a company called VisualDNA says, "We collect information about demographics, intent, interests, and personality. These

can predict what people might be interested in buying or hearing about." What are examples of how this information is used? How does it affect you?

8. According to the *BBC News* article, many Facebook quizzes install an app that continues to run in the background collecting your Facebook data long after you have finished a quiz. What do you think about this? Is it important to limit third-party access to your information? Why or why not? What can you do to prevent third-party apps from collecting your data?

9. After reading these articles and participating in the discussion, will you be more likely or less likely to answer online quizzes? Why or why not?

2. Protecting student data in schools

Jennifer Colby

You (and your students) are a data goldmine. Whether taking an assessment, checking out a library book, or even just showing up to school — information is collected, analyzed, disseminated, and studied to determine how to make future decisions. But who is looking at this data? Who is that information shared with? Entities outside of your school also have access to your data, especially if you take a state or national standardized test, have a Google G Suite account, or use an app for a classroom activity. Some states have laws protecting student data and some do not. Understanding that your data is collected, shared, and used if the first step of knowing how to better protect your personal information.

Resources

Barnes, Khaliah. 2014, "Student Data Collection Is Out of Control." *New York Times*, December 19. Accessed June 6, 2017. http://www.nytimes.com/roomfordebate/2014/09/24/protecting-student-privacy-in-online-learning/student-data-collection-is-out-of-control . (Browse a few editorial viewpoints.)

Breitenbach, Sarah. 2016. "States Scramble to Protect Student Data and Privacy." *PBS*, June 9. Accessed June 6, 2017. http://www.pbs.org/newshour/rundown/states-scramble-to-protect-student-data-and-privacy/ .

Camera, Lauren. 2015. "New California Law Limits Use of Student Data." *U.S. News and World Report*, December 29. Accessed June 6, 2017. https://www.usnews.com/news/articles/2015-12-29/new-california-law-limits-use-of-student-data .

"A Special Report on Student-Data Privacy." 2015. *Education Week*, October 21. Accessed June 6, 2017. http://www.edweek.org/ew/collections/student-data-privacy-special-report/ . (Browse a few articles).

Discussion questions

1. What is student data? Brainstorm a list of the types of personal information students share in their daily lives at school.

2. What are ways that student data is collected? What kinds of systems collect data, and for what purposes? Brainstorm a list of the ways that faculty, administration, or students might share student data while engaging in school activities.

3. Is it important to protect student data? Why or why not? For how long after a student leaves should data be kept and protected?

4. Do you know of any ways that your school protects your data? If yes, what are they? If no, how could you find out?

5. What is meant by the term "third-party"? How does official student data end up in the hands of third parties?

6. What is meant by "aggregating" data? Does aggregated data make you feel better about sharing of student data beyond the district level? Why or why not?

7. Navigate to this article: http://www.ncsl.org/research/education/student-data-privacy.aspx and find your state in the "Student Data Privacy" map. Does your state have a law (legislative enactment) to protect student data? If yes, what year were laws enacted? What do the laws require? Allow?

8. Consider the *U.S. News and World Reports* article. The state of California has the most rigorous law protecting student data. What makes it more stringent than the laws protecting student data in other states? Is that an advantage or disadvantage? How might your answer change if you were thinking like a school or district administrator, a state agency head, a family, or an individual student?

9. Do you think there should be a national law to protect student data, or do you think those protections should continue to occur at the state level? Why?

3. SAT and ACT information: What happens to it?

Jennifer Colby

More and more states are requiring high school students to take a college-admissions exam (SAT or ACT) in order to satisfy national education requirements. But if you have ever taken one of these tests, you know that all that bubbling in takes a long time as you answer questions about "geographic, attitudinal and behavioral information" (College Board 2017). The vast amounts of personal information gathered about students who take these tests is used for many purposes. The information can be used to design more fair and equitable tests, but it can also be accessed and analyzed by third-parties. Whether you are a student or an educator, did you ever wonder why this information is collected and what is done with it?

Resources

"ACT Privacy Policy." 2015. ACT, INC., March 31. Accessed June 6, 2017. http://www.act.org/content/act/en/privacy-policy.html .

College Board, The. 2017. "College Board Search." Accessed May 20, 2017. https://collegeboardsearch.collegeboard.org/pastudentsrch/login.action?excmpid=OC218-PR-05-TW .

"Five Principles to Protect Student Privacy." 2008. *Parent Coalition for Student Privacy*. Accessed June 6, 2017. https://www.studentprivacymatters.org/five-principles-to-protect-study-privacy/ .

"Our Commitment to Your Privacy." 2016. The College Board, January 15. Accessed June 6, 2017. https://www.collegeboard.org/privacy-policy .

Strauss, Valerie. 2017. "How the SAT and PSAT Collect Personal Data on Students – and What the College Board Does with It." *Washington Post*, March 30. Accessed June 6, 2017. https://www.washingtonpost.com/news/answer-sheet/wp/2017/03/30/how-the-sat-and-psat-collect-personal-data-on-students-and-what-the-college-board-does-with-it/ .

Discussion questions

1. National assessments such as the PSAT/SAT and the ACT Aspire/ACT ask for personal information about the student. What do you remember about the kinds of information you have been asked for when taking one of these tests?

2. How is this information used by The College Board and ACT? Why do you think this information is collected? What are third parties? What are examples of third parties?

3. Consider the "All States" chart in this link: http://www.edweek.org/ew/section/multimedia/states-require-students-take-sat-or-act.html . What "high school test" does your state offer? Are you *required* to take it? How do you think mandatory use of these tests, which used to be taken only by those who wanted to continue on to college post-graduation, has changed now that they are mandatory in some states? What do you think about your state's requirements compared to others?

4. What are the benefits of personal information collection as identified by The College Board? Have you used any of the services identified? If so, have they been helpful?

5. What do you think about The College Board's claim of information collecting being optional? If you have taken the PSAT/SAT or the ACT Aspire/ACT, what was your experience?

6. What are the "Five Principles to Protect Student Privacy" from the Parent Coalition for Student Privacy (PCSP) website? What is your reaction to them?

7. Compare the privacy policies of both The College Board and ACT with the PCSP's "Five Principles to Protect Student Privacy." How do the testing institution's practice comply with the Five Principles? How do they differ?

8. Consider how the answers in the "emailed response" received from The College Board in the *Washington Post* article compare with its privacy policy. Does the response from The College Board align with its policy? Why or why not? Compare the privacy policies of The College Board and the ACT. How are they the same? How are they different?

4. Surveillance cameras in schools and the case of special education

Susan Smith

Surveillance video is increasingly used in public spaces like intersections, parking lots, and entrances to deter and detect criminal behavior. The vast majority of schools in the U.S. have cameras in parking lots or at entrances, but how do we feel about cameras in the classroom?

Students, teachers, and parents have conflicting concerns. We applaud surveillance technologies when they catch criminals and protect children, but when cameras violate our civil rights and change our school climate, it gives rise to debate over who and what gets recorded and who gets to review the archived video footage.

Special education classrooms are a protected population for whom some parents feel security cameras are essential. Texas was the first state to pass a bill, effective in 2016, that required cameras in all special education classrooms. Las Vegas has a similar bill up for vote in 2017. Is this surveillance justified, or will it pave the way for increased surveillance in all classrooms?

Resources

Cardoza, Kavitha. 2017. "Will Classroom Cameras Protect Students with Special Needs?" 2017. *PBS NewsHour*. Accessed June 6, 2017. http://www.pbs.org/newshour/bb/will-classroom-cameras-protect-studentsspecial-needs/ .

Exter, Monty. 2015. "Cameras in the Classroom: FAQs on Senate Bill 507." *TeachTheVote*, July 15. Accessed June 11, 2017. http://www.teachthevote.org/news/2015/07/15/cameras-in-the-classroom-faqs-on-senate-bill-507/ .

Jenne, Inc. 2017. "Making the Case for Security Cameras in Schools and Colleges." *Business Solutions*. Accessed June 6, 2017. https://www.bsminfo.com/doc/making-the-case-for-security-cameras-in-schools-and-colleges-0001 . (account required)

Kille, Leighton W. and Martin Maximino. 2014. "The Effect of CCTV on Public Safety: Research Roundup." *Journalistsresesouce.org*, February 11. Accessed June 6, 2017. https://journalistsresource.org/studies/government/criminal-justice/surveillance-cameras-and-crime .

Kudialis, Chris. 2017. "Advocates Push Bill Calling for Video Cameras in CCSD Special Ed Classrooms." *Las Vegas Sun*, March 8. Accessed June 6, 2017. https://lasvegassun.com/news/2017/mar/08/advocates-bill-video-cameras-special-ed-classrooms/ .

Rapp, David. 2017. "Privacy vs. Security." *Scholastic*. Accessed June 6, 2017. http://www.scholastic.com/browse/article.jsp?id=3751958 .

Samuels, Christina A. 2016. "Cameras in Special Ed. Classrooms a Complex Issue." *Education Week*, September 20. Accessed June 6, 2017. http://www.edweek.org/ew/articles/2016/09/21/cameras-in-special-ed-classrooms-a-complex.html .

Steketee, Amy M. 2012. "The Legal Implications of Surveillance Cameras." *DistrictAdministration*, January 26. Accessed June 6, 2017. https://www.districtadministration.com/article/legal-implications-surveillance-cameras .

Walker, Tim. 2015. "Cameras in the Classroom: Is Big Brother Evaluating You?" *NEAToday*, January 23. Accessed June 6, 2017. http://neatoday.org/2015/01/23/cameras-in-the-classroom-big-brother-evaluating/ .

Discussion questions

1. What issues are we trying to solve with cameras? Have the laws in Texas and Nevada adequately defined acceptable use of the the surveillance cameras?

2. Is video surveillance in the classroom justified? Under what circumstances or for which populations?

3. Since surveillance cameras are an expensive purchase for any school district, who should decide if the expense is justified, when it necessarily comes at the cost of other educational services or tools?

4. Before installing classroom surveillance systems, districts must clearly identify objectives and intended outcomes. How could video recording benefit teachers? Students? Parents? Who should be informed?

5. If classroom video is collected, how long should it be retained? Should cameras collect video only? What are the advantages and disadvantages of recording both audio and video? (You might find it useful to review your state's laws on recording and consent prior to discussing this question.)

6. Who should have access to the recordings? Under what circumstances?

7. Under what circumstances might the recordings be used for teacher training? Teacher evaluation?

8. Are classrooms places where students and staff should expect privacy? If your school installed cameras in classrooms, what kind of atmosphere would it create at your school? How would it affect school climate?

9. Should video recordings of students be considered "student records" and, as a result, fall under FERPA protection? How should schools handle inquiries from media or law enforcement about surveillance footage? Should these be considered "public records" that fall under the Freedom of Information Act?

10. Once installed for other reasons, how might administrators use surveillance cameras to monitor staff? What might be the unintended consequences or benefits of surveillance cameras in classrooms?

5. Student privacy in the age of cloud storage

Susan Smith

As cloud-based services become more popular in schools, privacy rights advocates question whether schools have the infrastructure and policies in place to adequately protect students. Fordham University released a report in 2013 suggesting public school districts large and small fail to protect data from student information systems, learning management systems, student performance, and classroom activities as they move to the cloud. Even when parents must set up accounts to access their own student's data, they don't realize that privacy protections from cloud services may be at odds with the District's privacy policy. The Family Educational Rights and Privacy Act (FERPA) protects education records, while the Children's Online Privacy Protection Act (COPPA) requires that parents be notified and consent to use of any student information collected by websites and games. Schools' agreements with cloud service providers often do not include data security; vendors can retain student information in perpetuity. Furthermore, teachers are encouraged to adopt ed tech tools in the classroom without support for how new apps and platforms rate when it comes to student privacy.

Resources

Alim, Frida, Nate Cardozo, Gennie Gebhart, Karen Gullo, and Amul Kalia. 2017. "Spying on Students: School-Issued Devices and Student Privacy." *Electronic Frontier Foundation*, April 13. Accessed June 6, 2017. https://www.eff.org/files/2017/04/13/student-privacy-report.pdf .

"Center on Law and Information Policy." *FLASH*. 2013. Accessed June 6, 2017. http://ir.lawnet.fordham.edu/clip/2/ .

"Congressional Committee Revives Data Security Legislation." 2009. CDT, May 18. Accessed June 6, 2017. http://www.cdt.org/legislation/105th/privacy/coppa.html . (Focus on Section M: *COPPA and Schools*. Does your school comply? How would parents or teachers verify?)

Davis, Michelle R. and Sean Cavanagh. 2014. "Cloud Computing in K-12 Expands, Raising Data Privacy Concerns." *Education Week*, January 7. Accessed June 6, 2017. http://www.edweek.org/ew/articles/2014/01/08/15cloud_ep.h33.html .

Gallagher, Kerry, Larry Magid, and Kobie Pruitt. 2016. "The Educator's Guide to Student Data Privacy." *ConnectSafely.org*, May 20. Accessed June 6, 2017. http://www.connectsafely.org/eduprivacy/ .

Discussion questions

1. Make a list of all of the online tools and services that a student accesses in your class. What do you make of this list?

2. How transparent is your school or district in sharing the privacy agreements with its cloud providers? Do parents have access to these agreements? Are they shared automatically, or only if they ask?

3. If you are a student, what information do you have about what kinds of data are collected about you?

4. If you want to use a new cloud based tool in your classroom, who "approves" its compliance with student privacy protection? How does this affect your willingness to use it?

5. What if the tool is suggested by a student? Selected at home by a student for use?

6. What if a tool is a consumer product rather than an explicitly educational app? Do you have your own criteria established when evaluating new educational apps for your classroom?

7. How can social media be used *safely* in the classroom? For what ages? For what purposes? Are there other tools that are less public that might meet similar goals?

8. After reviewing "Congressional Committee Revives Data Security Legislation" above, do you think sites like Amazon and GoodReads comply with COPPA in regard to publishing student reviews? What loopholes might the companies exploit?

9. How would you initiate a discussion among staff at your school about protecting student privacy? Who would you choose as allies?

10. How would you initiate a similar discussion with parents or students? Consider the parent voices in the Electronic Frontier Foundation reading above as you discuss options.

6. Big Data and government nudges

Debbie Abilock

Big Data is being used to better understand behaviors and preferences – in medicine, economics, and other fields. Governments use behavioral insights to help people make better choices that also serve government goals. Healthier people + healthier communities = less government money spent on health problems.

Recognizing that people's choices are affected by unconscious flaws in reasoning like confirmation bias, some government agencies engineer social outcomes through easy and cheap "nudges" to encourage people to make choices in their (and society's) best interests. Called *libertarian paternalism*, the goal is to "alter people's behavior in a predictable way without forbidding any options or significantly changing their economic incentives" (Thaler & Sunstein 2009, 58). For example, because my local government officials in Palo Alto, California, are aware from Big Data reports that an estimated ¼ of all food calories produced in the world are lost or wasted (Lipinsky et al 2013), the town now provides each household with a plastic kitchen bucket labeled with the kinds of food scraps that can be composted. This nudge free to me as a citizen and economical for the city's zero-waste initiative — there is no penalty if I choose not to comply.

Proponents welcome small nudges as a temperate way of framing good choices, creating incentives that improve people's lives without coercion. Critics decry nudges as unconscious manipulation and question how sure one can be, given the lack of scientifically tested research, that these are the right solutions to complex problems.

This case study looks at the nature of government nudges which arise from Big Data correlations and examines their effectiveness in addressing predictive assumptions about obesity and health.

Resources

Democratic Audit UK. 2015. "'Nudges' May Be Effective at Times, but Policymakers Will Be Disappointed if They Rely on Them to Tackle Entrenched Problems." *Democratic Audit UK*, April 21. Accessed June 30, 2017. http://www.democraticaudit.com/2015/04/21/nudges-may-be-effective-at-times-but-policymakers-will-be-disappointed-if-they-rely-on-them-to-tackle-entrenched-problems/ .

Dobbs, Richard, Corinne Sawers, Fraser Thompson, James Manyika, Jonathan Woetzel, Peter Child, Sorcha McKenna, and Angela Spatharou. 2014. "How the World Could Better Fight Obesity." *McKinsey Report*, November. Accessed June 30, 2017. http://www.mckinsey.com/industries/healthcare-systems-and-services/our-insights/how-the-world-could-better-fight-obesity .

Harmon, Katherine. 2011. "Does Calorie-Labeling at Restaurants Lead to Healthier Eating?" *Scientific American*, January 14. Accessed June 30, 2017. https://www.scientificamerican.com/article/calorie-labeling-menus/ .

O'Connor, Anahad. 2016. "How the Government Supports your Junk Food Habit." *New York Times*, July 19. Accessed June 30, 2017. https://well.blogs.nytimes.com/2016/07/19/how-the-government-supports-your-junk-food-habit/ .

Oliver, Adam. 2014. "Nudging the Obese." *The London School of Economics and Political Science*, July 7. Accessed June 30, 2017. http://www.lse.ac.uk/researchAndExpertise/researchHighlights/Health/NudgingTheObese.aspx .

Petrescu, Dragos C., Gareth J. Hollands, Dominique-Laurent Couturier, Yin-Lam Ng, Theresa M. Marteau. 2016. "Public Acceptability in the UK and USA of Nudging to Reduce Obesity: The Example of Reducing Sugar-Sweetened Beverages Consumption." *PLOS ONE*, May 6. Accessed June 30, 2017. http://journals.plos.org/plosone/article/file?id=10.1371/journal.pone.0155995&type=printable .

Schubert, Christian. 2016. "A Note on the Ethics of Nudges." *Vox*, January 22. Accessed June 30, 2017. http://voxeu.org/article/note-ethics-nudges .

Smith, Eileen. 2016. "Chile Battles Obesity with Stop Signs on Packaged Foods." *NPR*, August 12. Accessed June 30, 2017. http://www.npr.org/sections/thesalt/2016/08/12/486898630/chile-battles-obesity-with-stop-signs-on-packaged-foods .

Discussion questions

1. Based on what you have read, how do you differentiate between a nudge and a regulation? Are they indistinguishable in practice?

2. You have read how governments are attempting to address Big Data's identified correlation between obesity and health. Under what circumstances do nudges appear to be more effective than laws and regulations?

3. What city, state, and local government nudges can you brainstorm that might impact obesity?

4. What criteria might you use to evaluate these government solutions – for example, using a ranking from high to low or a SWOT analysis (e.g., easy/hard implementation and limited/large impact)?

5. What nudges could be implemented by more than one governmental entity (local, state or national)? What delicious and healthy "smoothie" of government nudges might you concoct to address this problem?

6. What are the trade-offs between personal autonomy and government paternalism? Nudges may be economical and easy but are they unethical?

7. Under what circumstances do you trust government to nudge you? Do you feel differently depending on which political party is in power?

Bibliography

Lipinsky, Brian, Craig Hanson, James Lomax, Lisa Kitinoja, Richard Waite, and Tim Searchinger. 2013. "Reducing Food Loss and Waste, Installment 2 of Creating a Sustainable Food Future." Working paper, World Resources Institute, Washington, DC, June. Accessed June 30, 2017. http://www.wri.org/sites/default/files/reducing_food_loss_and_waste.pdf.

Thaler, Richard H., and Cass R. Sunstein. 2009. *Nudge: Improving Decisions about Health, Wealth, and Happiness*. Rev. exp. ed. New York: Penguin Books.

7. The fear factor: Hyped-up use of data to sway public opinion/behavior

Susan D. Ballard

With increasing regularity, data is used/misused to create a heightened sense of urgency related to any number of social, environmental, and health concerns. Examples include hyped-up media coverage related to such issues as: the "Millennium Bug" (or Y2K computer flaw) where there was minimal if any impact; a never realized world-wide outbreak of bird flu; and inflated claims that violence in video games leads to the development of violent personalities.

There are also examples of using data to sway public opinion such as the claim that significant numbers of "weapons of mass destruction" justified the U.S. invasion of Iraq. Additionally, the emergence of social media as a news source with citizen journalists reporting has intensified the "fear factor," spurring an unprecedented immediacy. An example is the use of social media to influence the "Brexit" decision in the United Kingdom.

In this case study, you'll learn more about how data and social-media-as-data is changing both journalism and the way global citizens interpret the current events and decisions around them.

Resources

American Institute of Physics (AIP) News Staff. 2014. "How Twitter Shapes Public Opinion." *AIP Publishing in the News*, March 11.

Retrieved June 16, 2017. https://publishing.aip.org/publishing/journal-highlights/how-twitter-shapes-public-opinion .

Gilman, Todd. 2015. "Media, Popular Culture, and Communication Rights Research Guide: Ethics & Watchdog Groups." *Yale University Library*, December 8. Retrieved June 6, 2017. http://guides.library.yale.edu/c.php?g=295905&p=1975646 .

Moeller, Susan. 2004. "Weapons of Mass Destruction and the Media: Anatomy of a Failure." *Yale Global Online*, April 14. Retrieved June 16, 2017. http://yaleglobal.yale.edu/content/weapons-mass-destruction-and-media-anatomy-failure .

Polonski, Vyacheslav. 2017. "Impact of Social Media on the Outcome of the EU Referendum." *Views from Oxford* (University of Oxford). Retrieved June 16, 2017. http://www.ox.ac.uk/news-and-events/oxford-and-brexit/brexit-analysis/views-from-oxford .

Sunne, Samantha. 2016. "Diving into Data Journalism: Strategies for Getting Started or Going Deeper." *American Press Institute*, March 9. Retrieved June 16, 2017. https://www.americanpressinstitute.org/publications/reports/strategy-studies/data-journalism/ .

Discussion questions

1. What do you know about journalistic and media integrity and ethics as it relates to journalism?

2. What about integrity and ethics as it relates specifically to the use of data?

3. "Fair and accurate" have been the long-time gold standard in reporting. In general, what is your analysis of the way data is used in reporting by the traditional mainstream media?

4. How does social media contribute to the "fear factor" in sharing data?

5. How can you distinguish between the hype about and the reality of an issue? Who or what are the sources that you rely on to know the difference?

6. *On the Media,* the public radio show about the role of journalism and the media in American life, has developed a series of Consumer's Handbooks related to emerging information. Visit http://www.wnyc.org/series/breaking-news-consumers-handbook and choose one of their handbooks to discuss in small groups. Which advice seems most important? Is anything missing? How might you share this information with others in your school or community?

8. Those smart devices are smarter than you think

Jennifer Colby

"Alexa", "Siri", "Ok Google" — these declarations are how we can get the attention of the smart devices that surround us. But did you realize that our smart devices are always at attention and vulnerable to hacking? We all benefit from these devices, but the pervasive use of them on our wrists, in our pockets, in our homes, and in our cars may make us susceptible to surveillance and tracking more than ever before. Recent news of CIA hacking into private citizens' phones, computers, and televisions may make us think twice about the benefits and drawbacks of using these devices and the connections they make between us and the outside world while passing along our personal information.

Resources

Chen, Brian X. 2017. "With C.I.A. Hacking Revelations, How to Protect Your Devices." *New York Times*, March 8. Accessed June 6, 2017. https://www.nytimes.com/2017/03/08/technology/personaltech/defense-against-cia-hacking.html .

Harris, Mark. 2016. "Virtual assistants such as Amazon's Echo break US child privacy law, experts say." *The Guardian*, May 26. Accessed May 23, 2017. https://www.theguardian.com/technology/2016/may/26/amazon-echo-virtual-assistant-child-privacy-law .

Lohr, Steve and Katie Benner. 2017. "With WikiLeaks Claims of C.I.A Hacking, How Vulnerable Is Your Smartphone?" *New York Times*, March 7. Accessed June 6, 2017.

https://www.nytimes.com/2017/03/07/technology/cia-hacking-documents-wikileaks-iphones-tvs.html .

"Marketing Your Mobile App: Get It Right from the Start." *Federal Trade Commission*. April 2013. Accessed June 6, 2017. https://www.ftc.gov/tips-advice/business-center/guidance/marketing-your-mobile-app-get-it-right-start .

McLaughlin, Eliott C. 2017. "Alexa, What Other Devices Are Listening to Me?" CNN, June 12. Accessed May 23, 2017. http://www.cnn.com/2017/01/12/tech/voice-technology-internet-of-things-privacy/.

Turner, Karen. 2016. "The Internet of Things Has a Privacy Policy." *Washington Post*, June 6. Accessed May 23, 2017. https://www.washingtonpost.com/news/the-switch/wp/2016/06/06/the-internet-of-things-has-a-child-privacy-problem/ .

Discussion questions

1. A smart device is an interactive electronic device that is wirelessly connected to other devices or networks. Brainstorm a list of smart devices that you own and/or have in your home.

2. Do you find smart devices beneficial to your life? Why or why not?

3. Now that it has been revealed that the CIA has hacked into personal smart devices, do you feel differently about using smart devices? Why or why not?

4. In regard to the news of CIA hacking into smart devices, WikiLeaks stated that it would redact and anonymize some

passages from the published documents. What does "redact" mean? What does "anonymize" mean? Is it important for WikiLeaks to redact and anonymize published information of this type? Why or why not?

5. What do you know about the privacy features or settings of your smart devices? Do you need to protect your smart devices from unwanted data collection? Why or why not? What can you do to protect your smart devices from unwanted data collection?

6. What is the purpose of the Children's Online Privacy Protection Act (COPPA)? List three ways in which COPPA protects collected data. Do you think COPPA is an effective measure to protect children? Does it go far enough or too far? Why or why not?

7. Who should be responsible for protecting the information that is collected by these smart devices? What is your reasoning? Should companies or parents be more responsible for protecting children's data?

9. Canaries in the mine: Chicago and Flint — haves vs. have-nots in use of data

Susan D. Ballard

In a tradition that lasted until the early part of the 20th century, canaries were carried into coal mines to detect carbon monoxide and other toxic gases before they could harm humans. The use of the phrase "like a canary in the mine" continues to be used to indicate when something is giving off early warning indicators that something is wrong and needs to be addressed. Similarly data can be harnessed as a means of providing insight and forewarning that certain products, systems, or behaviors have negative impact. The data can help drive potential solutions or avoidance measures. However, sometimes, the data is not utilized and/or ignored.

Throughout this book, you've read examples of projects in which better data is linked with better outcomes. In this case study, we'll examine what happens when data points to a problem that is *not* addressed.

Resources

Epton, Abraham, Alex Bordens, and Geoff Hing. 2015. "Chicago Lead Poisoning Rates Vary by Location, Time." *Chicago Tribune*, May 1. Accessed May 14, 2017. http://apps.chicagotribune.com/news/watchdog/chicago-lead-poisoning/ .

Fredrickson, Leif. 2016. "The Surprising Link Between Postwar Suburban Development and Today's Inner-City Lead Poisoning." *Conversation*, February 25. Accessed June 16, 2017.

https://theconversation.com/the-surprising-link-between-postwar-suburban-development-and-todays-inner-city-lead-poisoning-54453 .

Hillenbrand, Katherine. 2017. "Boston's Citywide Analytics Team: Leading the Way to a Data-Driven City." *Data-Smart City Solutions*, May 15. Accessed June 16, 2017. http://datasmart.ash.harvard.edu/news/article/case-study-bostons-citywide-analytics-team-1043 .

Ingraham, Christopher. 2016. "This is How Toxic Flint's Water Really Is." *Washington Post*, January 15. Accessed July 8, 2017. https://www.washingtonpost.com/news/wonk/wp/2016/01/15/this-is-how-toxic-flints-water-really-is/?utm_term=.9eaad0b1d5ea .

Parks, Jeffrey and Anurag Mantha. 2015. "Lead Testing Results for Water Sampled by Residents: Flint Has a Very Serious Lead In Water Problem." *Flint Water Study*, September. Accessed July 8, 2017. http://flintwaterstudy.org/information-for-flint-residents/results-for-citizen-testing-for-lead-300-kits/ .

Lead Safe Illinois. 2017. "Ripple Effects of Childhood Lead Poisoning." *Lead Safe Illinois*. Accessed June 16, 2017. http://www.leadsafeillinois.org/facts/ripple-effects.asp .

Teaching With Data. 2016. "The Data of the Flint Water Crisis." TeachingWithData.org, April 6. Accessed July 10, 2017. http://teachingwithdata.blogspot.com/2016/04/the-data-of-flint-water-crisis.html .

Discussion questions

1. Is there a pattern of dereliction of duty by decisionmakers when data results are confined to or affecting low socioeconomic communities versus middle and upper classes?

2. Do you think that government would be more responsive if the data showed unacceptable conditions in middle- or upper-class communities instead of poor ones? Why or why not?

3. Should citizens have a right to receive information and data from the government in order to participate in decisions about activities that impact the environment and health? Should more government data be made available to citizens so they can identify challenges and propose solutions? What kinds of supports would need to be in place so citizens would know how and where to access that data?

4. How can successful initiatives like Boston's Citywide Data Analytics Team be replicated in other communities? What, according to Hillenbrand's article, do you see as the factors contributing to their success?

5. How can communities be mobilized to help to gather and use data to improve services?

6. What can you do in your community to use data to ensure citizen health and safety and improve the quality of life?

7. Is data always the most persuasive tool citizens and government officials have in their toolkit? What other types of arguments, efforts, or activism have traditionally been successful? When might data be the least effective type of argument?

10. The implications of privacy regulation on Internet privacy

Tyler Hoff

In response to the repeal of new Internet privacy regulations (see pages 101-103), many Americans have taken a larger interest in securing their Internet privacy. Many people have turned to a variety of workarounds to protect their privacy. These include proxy servers, which are intermediaries between a user and content to limit and organize requests for that content, and are not necessarily encrypted; Virtual Private Networks (VPNs), which are encrypted networks allowing users to access resources and services while not in a specific physical location; and other privacy workarounds like Tor, which stands for The Onion Router, is a secure method of accessing the Internet anonymously, and is also used to access "the dark web," unindexed parts of the Internet mostly home to illegal or unethical activity. The following resources and discussion questions are intended to help a group explore the practical and ethical implications of using such tools.

Resources

Chen, Brian X. 2017. "For Internet Privacy, VPNs Are an Imperfect Shield." *New York Times*, April 5. Accessed May 30, 2017. https://www.nytimes.com/2017/04/05/technology/personaltech/vpn-internet-security.html .

Fung, Brian. 2017. "The Inventor of the Web Predicts 'A Massive Outcry' Over Online Privacy." *Washington Post*, April 4. Accessed 30 May, 2017. https://www.washingtonpost.com/news/the-switch/wp/2017/04/04/the-inventor-of-the-web-explains-why-you-shouldnt-use-a-vpn/ .

Larson, Quincy. 2017. "Set Up a VPN in 10 Minutes for Free — and Yes, Americans Urgently Need One, Thanks to Congress." *Quartz*, March 29. Accessed May 30, 2017. https://qz.com/945261/how-to-get-a-personal-vpn-and-why-you-need-one-now/?utm_source=readnext .

Sponsored Internet. 2017. "2017 ISP Privacy Regulations in the United State: All You Need to Know." *Techradar*, April. Accessed May 30, 2017. http://www.techradar.com/news/2017-isp-privacy-regulations-in-the-united-states-all-you-need-to-know .

U.S. Congress. Senate. Joint Resolution. S. Res. 34. 199th Cong., 1st sess., (December 2, 2016): S1. Accessed June 9, 2017. https://www.congress.gov/115/bills/sjres34/BILLS-115sjres34enr.pdf .

Wolff, Josephine. 2017. "Congress Will Let Internet Providers Sell Your Data — So Rebels Devised a Way to Fool Corporations." *Quartz*, April 3. Accessed May 30, 2017. https://qz.com/948340/congress-will-let-internet-providers-sell-consumer-data-so-rebels-devised-a-way-to-trick-corporations/ .

Discussion questions

1. Proxy servers are an oft-used tool to get around firewalls at schools and businesses that monitor and restrict onsite Internet activity. Considering the new focus on Internet privacy, is using such tools ethical when located in such a business or school? What about more generally?

2. Virtual Private Networks, or VPNs, are legal tools in the United States that can allow you to circumvent surveillance from your ISP. However, some can slow your Internet connection, and the best ones cost a monthly fee. Are they worth it for your average consumer?

3. VPNs can also monitor your web traffic in much the same way an ISP could, and are not required to keep that data private. Does this change your answer?

4. In an April 2017 article for *Quartz* (above), Josephine Wolff wrote about ways citizens were "rebelling" against this legislation. They designed a series of tools to create artificial searches in your search engine or Facebook feed to disguise your preferences. Their goal is to create more Internet "noise" to make it harder for ISPs and companies to create an accurate sense of who you are. However, Wolff admits these noise generators may not be able to override algorithms. They also generate additional traffic that may overwhelm servers that host websites. Are such efforts ethical? How do you determine the morality of such moves? Does this problem solve a problem or create new ones? How do you decide?

5. Tor can be used to access parts of the Internet that are mostly used for unscrupulous activity. If more people start using Tor to access the Internet, do you think more people will start accessing the dark web? Will illegal web activity increase? How would improved access for most people affect the contents of the dark web?

6. In an interview with the *Washington Post* (see link above), Tim Berners-Lee, the inventor of the Internet, argues that you should not use VPNs and similar privacy tools as a method of protest to ensure that privacy on the web remains accessible to all people. Is this a "good" argument? Why or why not? What arguments can one make that this is (or is not) an effective method of action?

7. Would you use any of the tools discussed above during your normal activity on the Internet? Why or why not? Would you recommend that other people use these tools, even if you do not want to?

NOTE: To continue your conversation on this topic, please see the case study "ISP consumer data collection," also written by Tyler Hoff, on pages 101-103.

11. Data philanthropy

Tasha Bergson-Michelson

Businesses sometimes come under fire for collecting a lot of information about individual clients and user behaviors and preferences. What if a business commits to sharing that information for the public good? This idea of "data philanthropy," which emerged in 2011 at the Davos World Economic Forum Annual Meeting, promotes the corporate world's ability to add significantly to the public good by donating to Big Data collections. The United Nations' Secretary General, António Guterres, has started the *Global Pulse* Big Data initiative that favors data philanthropy.

Already, fields like health, humanitarian aid, and disaster relief have benefited from data donations. But the story is not purely a rosy one: if there are questions about the ethics of businesses tracking customers and their behavior in the first place, does donating it to a global cause change that picture?

Resources

Coren, Michael J. 2011. "Data Philanthropy: Open Data for World-Changing Solutions." *Fast Company*, Dec. 12. Accessed June 27, 2017. https://www.fastcompany.com/1678963/data-philanthropy-open-data-for-world-%20changing-solutions .

Hasenkopf, Chris. 2017. "The Risk of Relying on 'Data Philanthropy' to Make Governments' Data Open." *OpanAQ.com*. April 12. Accessed June 27, 2017. https://medium.com/@openaq/the-risk-of-relying-on-data-philanthropy-to-make-governments-data-open-269be442c1f6 .

Pawelke, Andreas and Anoush R. Tatevossian. 2013. "Data Philanthropy: Where Are We Now?" *United Nations Global Pulse*, May 8. Accessed June 27, 2017. http://www.unglobalpulse.org/data-philanthropy-where-are-we-now .

Stempeck, Matt. 2014. "Sharing Data Is a Form of Corporate Philanthropy." *Harvard Business Review*, July 24. Accessed June 27, 2017. https://hbr.org/2014/07/sharing-data-is-a-form-of-corporate-philanthropy .

Taddeo, Mariarosaria. 2017. "Data Philanthropy and Individual Rights." *Minds & Machines* 27, (2017) : 1-5. Accessed June 27, 2017. http://paperity.org/p/79350540/data-philanthropy-and-individual-rights .

Discussion questions

1. Why might a company want to donate its data? What are the advantages and disadvantages for the company?

2. Sometimes companies are donating their own data, but sometimes they are using their resources and skill sets to make existing public data (gathered from governments or other organizations that cannot do it themselves) more accessible to others. What are the implications for a company making someone else's data available to the public?

3. Can it hurt people if companies donate their data in aggregate? In what ways?

4. The United Nations has been considering the ethics of data philanthropy. They see four potential ways for companies to share user data:

- » Share aggregated data to try and protect individual users;
- » Have independent researchers go into many companies and look at each company's data separately, behind that company's firewall;
- » Partner groups of competitors together and have them all contribute their data to aggregate datasets, so no one gets a competitive advantage; or
- » Let companies analyze their own data and give them guidelines for when to alert an independent organization that something is happening that needs attention.

Which of these methods do you think would be most useful, based on all you have learned about Big Data, ethics, and protection of personal information? What are the strengths and pitfalls of each?

5. A really interesting example of a private organization paying for and creating systems for sharing government data is USAFacts.org. Funded by former Microsoft CEO Steve Ballmer, USA Facts attempts to first bring together data from over 60 U.S. government agencies and, secondly, to demonstrate visually and interactively the sources of U.S. revenue (e.g., taxes) and how those taxes are spent (federal budget). Now that Ballmer has provided this valuable resource, what are his ethical obligations to the public to maintain it?

6. One of the things that USA Facts attempts to do is make government data easier to find and more accessible. Think back to Question 2 above, which posed a similar scenario in which a company is "packaging" existing data from another source. Does the addition of navigation tools or other

features to an existing dataset fundamentally change that dataset? For example, if it's easier to browse or look for information inside a dataset, does that fundamentally change the potential impact of sharing the data, either for positive or negative reasons?

Appendix A: Data literacy rules of thumb

These rules of thumb are culled from Cherry Lake Publishing's Data Geek series, a collection of middle-grade books that focus on data and statistical literacy, reading and writing data in arguments, data visualization, big data, citizen science, personal data management, and ethical data use.

Consider using these as "Data of the Week" discussion prompts in class, during advisory periods, on school displays, and more.

Data and statistical literacy

- » If you know the language of statistics, you will have a deeper understanding of what they mean.
- » There are three ways of calculating averages: mean, median, and mode. When you see the word "average," ask, "Which average do they mean?"
- » A bunch of statistics is called a dataset. A single number in that group is called a data point.
- » When one data point seems out of the range of the other points, it's called an outlier. Be careful making too many assumptions when you have outliers.
- » Good questions to ask when you find data include:
    - Who gathered and measured the statistic? Are they are a reliable source?
    - What is being measured? How was it measured? What information might have been left out?
    - Where did the information come from? Look for a citation or source.
    - When was the data collected? Is it still current? Is it historic data?

- Why would you use this — and not other — data?
- How was the data collected?

» Government websites are traditionally an unbiased source of information.

» Statistical benchmarks are known numbers that we can compare new numbers to. For example, there are about 325 million people in the United States. Now that you know that information, you can better understand what it means that Michigan has about 10 million residents.

» Be careful when comparing statistics that they are measuring the same thing!

Reading and writing data in arguments

» Using accurate data makes your claims stronger.

» Credible data can help people advocate for or make better decisions.

» People can accidentally or purposefully manipulate statistics.

» When you see data and statistics in newspapers, websites, or magazine articles, ask, "Is this a credible source?"

» There can be many ways to represent your data. Choose one that is both accurate and helps people understand the data better.

» Use data as evidence to support your argument or claim.

» Don't assume that people will know what your data means. Explain it!

Understanding data visualizations

- » In general, a single map, graph, or chart is considered a visualization.
- » When you combine sets of facts, numbers, statistics, and/or visualizations, you create an infographic. Check that pie chart segments add up to 100%.
- » When the colors of a pie chart are too similar, you can accidentally imply that the slices are related to one another.
- » Don't have so many pie chart slices that the audience gets confused.
- » 3D charts can be misleading by making parts of the chart seem larger or smaller than they are.
- » Always check the interval (the distance between points) on graphs.
- » Consider how a chart's design choices are intended to make you feel.
- » Pay attention to where axes start and end.
- » Don't assume either axis starts at 0.
- » Ask yourself, "Who made the infographic, and why?"
- » Ask yourself, "What is the purpose of this infographic?"
- » Ask yourself, "What do the individual parts of the data visualization represent?"
- » Ask yourself, "What elements are being considered by the labels of the chart?"
- » Look at the directions, sizes, lengths, width, colors and shapes of elements. What do they indicate?

Creating data visualizations

- » Visualizations aren't new — think of ancient Egyptian hieroglyphs that were used to communicate troop strength, crop size, or royal hierarchy.
- » Use a visualization or infographic to add value and improve meaning, not just to make something pretty.
- » Good visualizations make something clearer to the reader than just a list of numbers would. You might have to try a few different formats to figure out which is best!
- » Label every element of a visualization.
- » Every good visualization has a message, even if it isn't said explicitly.
- » Know what you are counting, so you know how to visualize it later.
- » Use pie charts only when everything you are counting is counted once.
- » When putting data on a map, use a range of a color (for example, light blue to dark blue) so viewers can see where data is larger. Make each gradation distinct.
- » Colors are powerful! If you are making a visualization about gender, then pink charts will automatically make many people think "female." Similarly, blue is traditionally the color of Democrats and red the color of Republicans. A chart with red and green may make some people assign stoplight values to your data!
- » Color sections gray on a map if you do not have data for them.
- » Use a key with labels so people know what each color, data point, or other information means.
- » Visualizing data should always enhance the meaning of the data.

Big Data

- » Big Data has the potential for us to discover new and valuable patterns.
- » Big Data is not necessarily good or bad.
- » Big Data helps generate very detailed information about customers, patients, or others. For example, stores create "personas" — imaginary profiles based on types of customers — to help them make decisions.
- » Data is being collected about you and your family, even if you do not realize it. For example, you may have a grocery store loyalty card that is tracking what you buy, what inventory to restock, or which coupons it should offer.
- » When you are offered something for free by a company, ask yourself, "What am I giving in order to receive this bonus?" You might be willing to give up the information in exchange for a good deal, but you also might not!
- » More data doesn't necessarily mean *better* or more accurate data. The programs that find patterns in data use formulas created by humans. Don't assume their outcomes are neutral information.
- » Like human decisions, Big Data can have unintended consequences.
- » Citizen science projects are similar to Big Data because many people contribute data and efforts to one project. Citizen science projects are generally considered to be helpful to people and nature.

Citizen science

- » Citizen science projects use volunteers to tag photos, take measurements, count objects, categorize data, make labels, or otherwise do analysis.

- » Some citizen "science" projects aren't about science at all. You can transcribe jokes, Civil War journals, or World War I letters, for example.
- » Citizen science projects can be in the wild or conducted from your computer screen.
- » Citizen science projects can help professional scientists find patterns and draw conclusions with more data, more speed, more variety, and at less cost.
- » Some citizen science projects are run not by professionals but by passionate amateurs.
- » Good planning and training help project organizers and volunteers know what to do, when to do it, and what information to share. Citizen science is only effective when everyone agrees on what to count, when to count it, and where to put the data.
- » For citizen science to be an effective way of gathering large amounts of data, everyone has to agree on what to count, when to count it, and where to put the data.
- » To find citizen science projects online, try sites like Zooniverse.org, SciStarter.com, Smithsonian Transcription (http://transcription.si.edu), Fold.it, or Journey North (http://learner.org/jnorth).

Personal data management

- » Personal information is information collected about us that might include age, height, weight, gender, address, phone number, email address, Instagram account, Social Security number, school information, report cards, criminal history, exercise levels, and more.
- » We need to make decisions about which information we share and which we keep private. We might not mind sharing our last name but want to keep our family's credit card numbers private.

- » Your Social Security number is likely your most private information. Keep it in a safe and secure place.
- » Identity theft or fraud can occur if private information gets into the wrong hands.
- » Encryption can help keep your online data safer.
- » Strong passwords can help keep your information safe.

Ethical data use

- » Ethics are our beliefs about what is good behavior, our sense of what is right and wrong.
- » Search carefully for trustworthy data. Consider the source of of the data.
- » Don't use data just because it supports your argument. That is known as "cherry picking."
- » Use ethically collected data.
- » Cite your data.
- » When you collect data, have a plan. If you change the plan, write that down.
- » You've heard people say, "don't compare apples and oranges." When making comparisons between data, make sure it is a fair comparison. For example, when you are comparing prices from 1957 to those from 2017, you need to take inflation into account.

Data literacy-related standards

The URL below provides data literacy-related standards compiled from the Common Core State Standards; Next Generation Science Standards; C3 Voluntary Social Studies Standards; and the *Standards for the 21st-Century Learner* (2007) from the American Association for School Librarians. This list should not necessarily be considered exhaustive, but may provide direction to link established Standards to data literacy instruction.

https://tinyurl.com/DataLiteracyRelatedStandards

Visit the following websites for additional information

Common Core State Standards Initiative
www.corestandards.org

Next Generation Science Standards
www.nextgenscience.org

C3 Voluntary Social Studies Standards
www.socialstudies.org

***Standards for the 21st-Century Learner*, American Association for School Librarians**
www.ala.org/aasl/standards/learning

Creating Data Literate Students

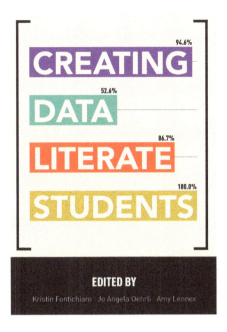

An additional title has also been created. In *Creating Data Literate Students* we concentrated on the nuts and bolts of modern data usage to provides high school librarians and educators with foundational domain knowledge to teach a new subset of information literacy skills — data and statistical literacy, including:

» statistics and data comprehension
» data as argument
» data visualization

Working in concert, these concepts can help librarians and educators make better sense of real-world data concerns and have the confidence and content knowledge to share those skills with the high schoolers they serve.

This title is available in print and Kindle formats at Amazon.com and in PDF and machine-readable formats at http://dataliteracy.si.umich.edu .

Contributors

Debbie Abilock co-founded and leads the education vision at NoodleTools, Inc., a teaching platform of integrated research tools for note-taking, outlining, citation, document archiving and annotation, collaborative research and writing. A *Library Journal* Mover and Shaker, she has worked on numerous local, state, and national boards and currently is on Granite State's (NH) National Advisory Board to create a new M.S. in School Leadership for future school principals, library media specialists, and experienced teachers that will blend online learning with extended supervised clinical experiences. Known for her innovative curriculum design and instructional strategies, she lectures and consults internationally. She co-authored a book on the varied professional development roles of school librarians (*Growing Schools*, Libraries Unlimited 2012) and served as founding editor of the AASL journal, *Knowledge Quest*. She writes "Adding Friction," a column about thoughtful teaching and learning, for *School Library Connection*. She contributed the chapter on professional development to *The Many Faces of School Library Leadership*, edited by Sharon Coatney and Violet H. Harada.

Susan D. Ballard is a Senior Lecturer and Program Director for the Master of Science in School Leadership Program (with School Library certification) at Granite State College of the University System of NH. She is a Past-President of AASL (2012-13) and the retired Director of Library, Media, and Technology Services for the Londonderry (NH) School District, a recipient of the National School Library Media Program of the Year (2000). She currently serves as a member of AASL's Standards and Guidelines Editorial Board and is a member of Julie Todaro's ALA Presidential Initiative Steering Committee. She is also a member of the Advisory Board for *Teacher Librarian*, the Board of Directors for the Q.E.D. Foundation, and the Leadership Council of the National Collaborative for Digital Equity. Susan has published numerous articles in a variety of professional and scholarly journals including one selected by the Library Instruction Round Table of ALA as one of the Top Twenty Library Instruction Articles of 2009. Among various awards, she was the first-ever recipient of the NH Excellence in Education Award (EDie) for Library Media Services.

Tasha Bergson-Michelson is the Instructional and Programming Librarian for Castilleja School in Palo Alto, California, where she builds curricula based on the notion that strong research skills lower the bar to curiosity. Since 1995, Tasha has been exploring what makes for successful information literacy instruction in corporate, non-profit, subscription, and school libraries, and through after school programs and summer camps. Most recently, Tasha was the Search Educator at Google, where she wrote an extensive series of Search Education lesson plans, the Power Searching MOOCs, and – most importantly – collaborated with other librarians around the world to explore the most effective ways of teaching research skills. In 2014 Tasha was designated a Mover and Shaker – Tech Leader by *Library Journal*.

Jennifer Colby is a High School Teacher Librarian at Huron High School in Ann Arbor, MI. She coordinates SAT training for students at her school and provides resources to help teachers integrate SAT skills into all content areas. She also works with students and teachers in her district to practice the skills necessary to take the Michigan Student Test of Educational Progress (M-STEP). In her spare time, she writes informational texts for elementary students.

Catherine D'Ignazio is an Assistant Professor of Data Visualization and Civic Media at Emerson College who investigates how data visualization, technology and new forms of storytelling can be used for civic engagement. Among other projects, Professor D'Ignazio co-created the Databasic platform and has conducted research on geographic bias in the news media, developed custom software to geolocate news articles and designed an application, "Terra Incognita," to promote global news discovery. She is working on sensor journalism around water quality with PublicLab, data literacy projects and various community-educational partnerships with her journalism students. Her art and design projects have won awards from the Tanne Foundation, Turbulence.org, the LEF Foundation, and Dream It, Code It, Win It. In 2009, she was a finalist for the Foster Prize at the ICA Boston. Her work has been exhibited at the Eyebeam Center for Art & Technology, Museo d'Antiochia of Medellin, and the Venice Biennial. Professor D'Ignazio is a faculty director at the Emerson Engagement Lab and a Research Affiliate at (and alumna of) the MIT Center for Civic Media.

Kristin Fontichiaro is a Clinical Associate Professor at the University of Michigan and principal investigator on the Supporting Librarians in Adding Data Literacy Skills to Information Literacy Instruction project (IMLS RE-00-15-0113-15). A *Library Journal* Mover and Shaker and member of the American Library Association's inaugural class of Emerging Leaders, she has written several books for educators, librarians, and K-12 readers.

Lynette Hoelter is an assistant research scientist and Director of Instructional Resources at ICPSR and a research affiliate of the Population Studies Center at the University of Michigan. At ICPSR, she is involved in projects focusing on assisting social science faculty with using data in the classroom, including the Online Learning Center and TeachingWithData.org, and generally oversees efforts focused on undergraduate education. Lynette is also a Co-Principal Investigator of the Integrated Fertility Survey Series, an effort to create a dataset of harmonized variables drawn from national surveys of fertility spanning 1955-2002. Her research interests include the relationship between social change and marital quality, gender in families, and the study of family and relationship processes and dynamics more broadly. She has also taught for the department of sociology and the survey methodology program at the University of Michigan.

Tyler Hoff is enrolled at the University of Michigan School of Information, and expects to graduate in the Spring of 2018. He primarily studies databases and information organization with a side of library studies, and is excited to be part of educating a new generation of more data literate and aware students.

Kelly Hovinga is enrolled in the Michigan School of Information, where she will be receiving a Master of Science in Information in 2018. She received a Masters in Art from the The Ohio State University for Russian History in 2014. We try not to hold it against her. Kelly currently works at the Stephen S. Clark Library in the rare maps collection.

Justin Joque is the Visualization Librarian at the University of Michigan. There he assists users in finding, manipulating, analyzing, and visualizing diverse types of data. Before becoming the Visualization Librarian, Justin was a Spatial and Numeric Data Librarian, also at the University of Michigan. He completed a Master's of Science of Information at the University of Michigan School of Information with a focus on Information Analysis and Retrieval and his Ph.D. in Communications at the European Graduate School.

Amy Lennex has worked in the publishing industry for nearly 20 years editing series nonfiction, middle-grade fiction, and picture books. She's also the author of *Personal Data Management*, part of the eight-book Data Geek series published by Cherry Lake Publishing. She provided project management and editing support for the Supporting Librarians in Adding Data Literacy Skills to Information Literacy Instruction project.

Jo Angela Oehrli is a former high school and middle school teacher who helps students find information on a wide range of topics as a Learning Librarian at the University of Michigan Libraries — Ann Arbor. In addition, she supports the students in the Women in Science and Engineering Residential Program and the students in the Michigan Research Community Residential Program as well as undergraduates across campus. She has published articles on library instruction, served as Chair of ALA LIRT's Top Twenty Committee, serves on the ACRL Instruction Section Executive Board & the LOEX Advisory Board, and has worked as an adjunct lecturer for UM's School of Information & the College of Literature, Science and the Arts. She also supports the research and instructional needs for those throughout the university community who are studying children's literature at any level.

Justin Schell is the Director of the Shapiro Design Lab, a peer learning and project design community at the University of Michigan Library. As a core member of the Data Rescue project, he has helped organize more than 40 events around the country since January 2017. He holds a Ph.D. from the University of Minnesota's Comparative Studies in Discourse Society, where he worked as part of the Digital Content Library and at the Immigration History Research Center. After completing his degree, he was a Council of Library and Information Resources Postdoctoral Fellow from 2013-2015 at the University of Minnesota Library. During his Fellowship, he developed and directed the DASH (Digital Arts Science + Humanities) program. In conjunction with the Givens Collection of African American Literature, he founded the Minnesota Hip-Hop Archive, a nearly 500-item collection of materials from the history of hip-hop in Minnesota. Schell is also a filmmaker and media artist. In addition to a number of short films, he directed *We Rock Long Distance*, a feature-length documentary film that weaves together the stories of three Minnesota hip-hop musicians with roots far beyond the "Land of 10,000 Lakes." He also did visual projections for the dance opera *Test Pilot*, about the Wright Brothers and their sister Katharine, in collaboration with composer Jocelyn Hagen and choreographer Penelope Freeh.

Jole Seroff is Director of Library and Information Services at Castilleja School in Palo Alto, California. She began her career in urban public schools in Memphis, Tennessee. She collaborates with faculty to infuse curriculum with research skills and a focus on intellectual freedom. She also implements humanities-based, hands-on learning through letterpress printing. She is lover of poetry, and works closely with student writers. In her free time, she enjoys birding, museums, and factory tours.

Susan Smith is Library Director at The Harker School in San Jose, California, where she has worked for 12 years. She holds an MLIS from San Jose State University, and a BA from Duke University. Smith oversees a team of seven professional librarians on four campuses, preschool through high school, where information literacy is embedded across the disciplines as librarians collaborate with teachers on hundreds of lessons each year. Teaching research skills in a rigorous college prep environment, Smith is committed to teaching data literacy to K-12 students and providing teachers with the professional development necessary to support such instruction. She frequently speaks at San Francisco Bay Area and national conferences on professional development, information literacy, and news literacy. Publications include co-authoring "An Argument for Disciplinary Information Literacy" in *Knowledge Quest* May/June 2016, and "Growing Information Literacy School-Wide," published in *Growing Schools: Librarians as Professional Developers*, edited by Debbie Abilock, Kristin Fontichiaro, and Violet Harada (Libraries Unlimited 2012).

Tierney Steelberg received her Master of Science in Information in 2016 from the University of Michigan School of Information, where she specialized in library and information science. She is currently the Instructional Technology Librarian at Guilford College.

Wendy Steadman Stephens is an Assistant Professor and School Library Program Chair at Jacksonville State University. A high school librarian for fifteen years, she earned National Board Certification in Library Media in 2008. A past president of the Alabama Library Association, she has served as ALA Councilor-at-Large, on the EMIERT Executive Board, and on the United States Board on Books for Young People Board of Directors, and was chosen as an ALSC Bechtel fellow in 2016. She has a Ph.D. from University of North Texas, and dissertation research focused on the interaction of reading practice and student attitudes surrounding literacy and libraries.

Martha Stuit is Reference Librarian at Delta College. She was the 2015-2016 project assistant on the Supporting Librarians in Adding Data Literacy Skills to Information Literacy Instruction project. She is a former reporter.

Samantha "Sam" Viotty is a multimedia artist and curriculum designer for social equity. A New York City native, she has always used urban landscapes and environments to ignite her creativity. Samantha is a staunch advocate for increased diverse representation in all sectors and this is the theme of her artistic and educational work. More recently, her work focuses on incorporating data in a creative way to further understand and combat social injustices. Sam's artistic career has revolved around youth and community work as a teaching artist, empowering youth to create and amplify their voice. She has worked on several projects over the past year that incorporate education, technology and creativity for social change, including DIY Data Literacy. Sam holds a Master of Arts in Civic Media, Art and Practice from the Engagement Lab at Emerson College, where she designed a creative data literacy curriculum for local public libraries.

Connie Williams is a National Board Certified Teacher Librarian and taught in junior high and high school libraries in Petaluma, California. She is a past president of the California School Library Association, a governor appointee to the California State Library Services Board, and a member of the ALA Government Documents Round Table Government Information for Children Committee. She has authored articles and chapters on school library advocacy, infographics, primary sources, and the Question Formulation Technique. Connie is an Adjunct Librarian and Instructor at the Santa Rosa Junior College and works at the Sonoma County Public Library. She blogs for *Knowledge Quest* at: http://knowledgequest.aasl.org/author/cwilliams/ .

Index

1Password 61
2016 election 34-37
3D charts 253
4T Virtual Conference on Data Literacy ii, iii, 8. *See also* Webinars.
4th Amendment 111-115, 190

A

Abilock, Debbie 50-54, 72-75, 159-169, 184-187, 230-233, 263
AboutMyInfo.org 94
Access 141, 151-154
ACLU. *See* American Civil Liberties Union.
ACT test 220-222. *See also* Standardized tests.
Action research 30-33
Activity trackers iv
Advertising 214
Analysis of 180-183
Advocacy 108-110
Adwords 201
AFP 128
African-American facial recognition 88
After-hours employee behavior 96
After-school programs 59
Aggregation of data 199-203, 218, 249
AI. *See* Artificial intelligence.
AirBnB 206
Airline tickets i
Alaska Native Science Commission 156
Alcoholic beverages 96
Alexa 90, 237
Algorithms i, iv, 87, 176, 188, 190, 199, 201, 210
    and race 88
Alim, Frida 227
Alito, Samuel 112
All Tech Considered 112, 117
Almanacs 23
Alternative knowledge 157
Amazon 86-88, 199, 227-229
Amazon Echo 86-88, 89-91, 237
Amazon Echo Look 86-88
Amazon.com 86-88, 199, 227-229, 237, 261
American Association of American Colleges and Universities 196
American Association of School Librarians 20-23, 259
American Civil Liberties Union (ACLU) 117, 189,209
American FactFinder (U.S. Census) 49
American Institute of Physics 234
American Press Institute 235
Analytics 201
Ancestry.com 93

Android 61
Angwin, Julia 98, 181
Animal identification 135-138
Anonymity online 57
Anonymized data 180-183, 238-239
Anonymous data, re-identification of 92
Apple 90, 111-115
Apple HomePod 86, 88, 89-91
Apple v. FBI 112, 113, 114, 115
Apple Watch 83-85, 91
Approval of third-party tools 227-229
Approval ratings, presidential 36
Apps 58-61
Apps marketing 237
AR. *See* Action research.
Archives 141
Archiving of federal data 151-154
Arctic Eider Society 156
Arctic weather 157
Area, Great Britain, 22
Area, U.S. 22
Arguments 52
Arizona v. Hicks 113
Arkansas 90
Arkansas murder case 89-91
Ars Technica 84, 101
Artifacts 139-141
Artifacts as data 139-141
Artificial intelligence 86-88, 188
Artificial turf and cancer 132, 133
Artist sketchbooks 139
    as seen by professionals 132-134
Assessment 43
Assessments 217. *See also* Standardized tests.
Associated Press 200
Astronomy 132, 160
At-risk students 195-198
Atlantic, The 205
Atlas Obscura 148
Audience for a letter 108-110
Audience measurement 180-183
Audubon Christmas Bird Count 167
Aurasma 144
Author's perspective 26
Auto insurance and vehicle monitoring devices 95-97
Automated driving 184-187
Autonomous trucks 184-187
Averages 9-12, 251
Axciom 199

B

Baby Boomers 116, 118
Back yards and citizen science 145-147, 167

"Backdoor "access to data 106, 118
Bailey, Tricia 124
Balancing liberties and security 113
Ballard, Susan D. 30-33, 62-64, 145-157, 195-198, 208-211, 234-236, 240-242, 263
Ballmer, Steve 249
Banking 192-194
Banks' behavior 176
Bar chart 44-46
Bar graph. *See bar chart*.
Barnes, Khallah 217
BBC News 215, 216
Beam online visualization tool 46
BeBusinessEd.com 108
Bejeweled game 136, 167
Benchmarking statistics. *See* Statistical benchmarks.
Benchmarks 52
Benner, Katie 237
Bergson-Michelson, Tasha 24-26, 86-88, 92-94, 108-110, 124-126, 247-250, 264
Berners-Lee, Tim 245
Bershidsky, Leonid 128
Bias 176-179. *See also* Discrimination.
   in the media 35
   cognitive 52
Biddle, Sam 172
Bies, Laura 146
Big Brother 225
Big Butterfly Count 167
Big Data ii, iv, v, 58, 98, 128, 155, 158, 171-211, 249, 255
   and "deep learning" 191
   and banking 192-194
   bias in 176-179
   and criminal sentencing 176
   and customer privacy 172-175
   and data philanthropy 247-250
   and discrimination 176-179, 189, 192-194, 195-198, 240-242
   and geospatial predictions 190
   and identification of individual criminals 190
   and junk food 231
   and marketing 192-194
   nudges 230-233
   and oversight 190
   and predictive analytics 195
   and real estate values 190
   and restaurant visits 190
   and stalking 208-211
   and surveillance 208
   and teacher expectations 195-198
   and tourism 190
Bigelow, William 83
Biodiversity 142-144, 145-147
Bird counting and tracking 167
Bird feeder monitoring 167

Bird flu 234
Bird migration 160
Birth rituals 155
Bloomberg 128
Blue-collar jobs, loss of 184
Body cameras 188
Bonaparte, Napoleon 207
Bordens, Alex 240
Boston Citywide Data Analytics Team 242
Boston, Mass. 241, 242
Boyd, Andrew 95
boyd, danah 57
Brandorn, Russell 101
Brands 16
Breakfast 16
Breitbart 83, 128
Breitenbach, Sarah 217
Brexit 127, 129, 234
Brill, Julie 193
British Broadcasting Company (BBC) 137, 215, 216
Broadcasts, in-school 16
Brodkin, Jon 101
Brogan, Jacob 177
Browsers 60
   activity within 58-61
   behavior noted in 199
   extensions for 61
   monitoring of 101-103
   sale of data from 244
Brunton, Finn 57
Bukszpan, Daniel 185
Burr-Feinstein de-encryption bill 105, 106
Bush, George W. 36, 103
Business Insider 96, 173, 189, 201, 202
Business Solutions 224
Butterfly projects in citizen science 132, 159, 167

C
C-science 159-169
Calendar reminders 61
California 122, 167, 219, 230
   roadkill in 133
California Academy of Sciences 163, 167
California Digital Library 151, 153
Calorie labeling in restaurants 231
Cambridge Analytica 127-130
Campbell-Dollghan, Kelsey 86
Canary in the mine 240
Cancer 116, 32, 133
Candy Crush 135-138
Canvassing 128
Car companies 192
Car insurance 97, 176
Car ownership data 127
Carbon monoxide 240
Cardoza, Kavitha 223
Cardozo, Nate 227

Career goals 80
Carnera, Lauren 218
Case studies iv-v, 32-33, 57-58, 77-250
Cash and privacy 98-100
Catalogs 64
Caucasian faces 88
Causation 9-12, 13-16, 24-26
    vs. correlation 9-12, 13-16
Cavanagh, Sean 228
CCTV. *See* Closed-caption television.
CDT.org 228
Cell mark-up 159
Cell nuclei, identification of 132
Cell phones 111-115. *See also* iPhones.
Census Explorer tool 49
Census, U.S. 22-23, 38-40, 47-49, 130, 178
Center for Democracy and Technology
    (CDT) 65-68, 104, 107
Center for Generational Kinetics 118
Center for Human Genetics 92
Center for Humans and Nature 136
Center for Identity 124
Center on Law and Information Policy 227
Central Intelligence Agency (CIA) 22-23,
    237-239
Central tendencies. *See* averages.
Charts 44-46, 253
Chasmar, Jessica 83
Chaves, Zoe 205
Chen, Brian X 237-239, 243
Chen, Michelle 205
Cherry Lake Publishing 251
Cherry-picking of data 22
Chewing gum 16
Chicago Tribune 240
Chicago 189, 240-242
Child privacy law 237
Child, Peter 231
Children's Online Privacy Protection Act
    (COPPA) 123, 227, 229, 239
Chile 232
Chintamaneni, Prasad 193
    choosing a classroom project in 159-
    169
Christian Science Monitor 125
Christopher S. Porrino v. Vizio, Inc. 181
Chrome browser 61
Chronicle of Social Change 209
CIA hacking 237-239
CIA World Factbook 22-23
Ciphers 104
Citation of data 257
Citizen epidemiology 134
Citizen science ii, iv, v, 72-75, 131-169,
    255-256
    and acknowledgement of
        contributors 134
    and assessment 141
    and backyard explorations 145-147
    and chat features 138
    and classroom curriculum 159-169
    and collaboration 73
    and community outreach 74
    and cultural understanding 139-141
    and definitions of success 162
    and educational goals 162
    and fashion advice 86-88
    and government agencies 154
    and habitats 145-147
    and hearings iii
    and humanities 139-141
    and leaf identification 142-144
    and levels of engagement 159-169
    and NASA 154
    and NOAA 154
    and outreach 161-162
    and pattern recognition 135-138
    and photographs 135-138
    and plant identification 142-144
    and prior knowledge 164-165
    and project portals 132, 165-166
    and project sources 165
    and protein folding 167
    and redundancy 162
    and scientific understanding 73
    and scope 163
    and search terms 168
    and Smithsonian 154
    and timing 165
    and training 161
    and transcription of documents
        139-141
    and user-added content 142-144
    and volunteer labor 132
    and warrants 89-91
    and wildlife 162
    prestige of 149
Citizenfour (film) 57
Citizenry, informed 17-19
CitizenScience.gov 166
Citizenship 17-19
    acts of 108-110
City analytics 241
City College of New York 143
Citywide Data Analytics Team (Boston)
    242
Civic analytics 241
Civic engagement 108-110
Civil liberties 111-114
Civil rights law 188, 189
Civil War soldier diaries 139
Civil War telegrams 159
Claims (as arguments) 52
Classroom surveillance 223-226
Clayton, Susan 136
Clickbait 26
Clickclickclick.click (website) 59-60
Clicks iv

Clinton, Hillary 36, 37
Close reading 24-26, 124-126
    of statistics 24-26
Closed-caption television (CCTV) 223-226
Clothing 86-88
Cloud computing 116
Cloud storage 188, 227-229
CNBC 112, 177, 185
CNN 80-81, 86, 238
Codes 104
Cognitive biases 52
Colby, Jennifer 17-19, 65-68, 80-82, 214-216, 217-219, 220-222, 237-239, 264
Collaborations between traditional and Western scientific knowledge 158
College admissions 80, 81, 196
College Board 220
College entrance exams 220-222
College goals 80
Color in data visualizations 39, 44-46, 254
Colorado University at Boulder 157
Columbia University 143
Combining data from multiple sources 199-203
Commerce Times 193
Commercials 16. *See also* Advertisements.
Common Core State Standards 259
Community organizations 42
Community outreach 74
Community use of data 41-43
Comparing statistics 252
Competitive Enterprise Institute 101
Composting 230
Computational thinking 27-29
Confessore, Nicholas 128
Confidence 13-16
Congress, U.S. 101-103, 244
Congress.gov 109
Congressional Review Act 103
Connected vehicle technology 184-187
Constitution, U.S. 111-115
Consumer benefits 101-103
Consumer data 64, 101-103, 127
    and 108-110
Consumer information 64
Consumer power 108-110
Consumer profiles 119
Consumer protection 60
Consumer spending 203
Consumer tracking 199-203
Consumer Watchdog 186
Consumer's Handbooks (*On the Media*) 236
Consumers and dynamic pricing 210
Content areas 17-19. *See also* Curriculum
Context for data 20-23
Control+F keystrokes 126
Controlling for ... 13-16
Conversation, The 240

Conversions 199-203
Converting to another visualization type 46
Cook, Tracy M. 95
Cooper, Daniel 86
COPPA. *See* Children's Online Privacy Protection Act.
Coren, Michael J. 247
Cornell Lab of Ornithology 145, 146, 164, 167
Cornell University Library 152
Corporate data donation 247-250
Corporate health strategies 95-97
Corporate philanthropy 247-250
Correlation 9-12, 13-16, 24-26
    vs. causation 9-12, 13-16
Coupons i
Couturier, Dominique-Laurent 232
Crawford, Kate 209
Creating Data Literate Students iii, 43, 261
Creative data literacy 41-43
Credible sources 252
Credit card companies 122
Credit card data 199-203
Credit fraud 194
Credit reports 64
Crime predictions 189
Crime prevention 188-191
Criminal behavior 99, 188-191
Criminal convictions 176
Criteria for preservation of data 69-71
Cross-conversion tracking 199-203
Cross-curricular data literacy 17-19
Cross-platform tracking 130
Crowdsourcing. *See* Citizen science.
Crump, Catherine 209
CTRL+F keystrokes 126
Cultural folklore and norms 155
Curriculum 10, 45, 59, 64
Cursive and transcription 149
Custom advertisements 127-128
Customer behaviors 199-203
Customer cards 63
Customer consent 180-183
Customer viewing history 180-183
Customized advertising 214
Cyberbullying 116

D
D'Ignazio, Catherine 41-43, 264
Daily observation 155
Daimler 184
Dark web 246
Data i
    access to 85
    analysis 41-43
    analytics 193. *See also* Data analysis.
    and discrimination 240-242
    and language 24-26

and public opinion 234-236
as evidence 20-23. *See also* Data in arguments.
at school 65-68
breaches 122-123
brokers of 127-130
capture of 210
collection 11, 39
comparison of 257
curation of 51-54
data collected 251
encrypted 104-107. *See also* Encryption
federal 65-68, 69-71
local 65-68
methods of 251
multidisciplinary nature of ii
neutrality of 39
techniques for 30-33
comprehension of iii, 17-19
dumps of 67
harvests of 151-154
in arguments iii, 17-19, 52, 252, 261
selection of 47-49
source of 27-29, 251
state-level 65-68
U.S. 69-71
Data Geek series 251
Data journalism 234-236
Data literacy 9-16, 20-23, 251
as mindset 9-16
in the content area 17-19
integration of 10
skills gap in 10
definition of i-ii, 9-16
reasons for 17-19
teaching of 38-40
Datasets 41-43
Data of the week strategy 11, 15, 29, 46, 251
Data philanthropy 247-250
Data plan of action 67
Data point, definition of 251
Data presentation 44-46
Data preservation 69-71, 210
Data privacy 118, 214-216, 256-257
and minors 123
Data Privacy Lab 92
Data Rescue events 69-71
Data sold to third parties 180-183
data sources ii
Data storytelling 41-43
Data visualization i, iii, 17-19, 34-37, 38-40, 41-43, 44-46, 47-49, 50-54, 253, 254, 261
and emotion 39
comprehension of 38-40
sources for 17-19
teaching of 38-40
scrapbooks of 40

types of 38-40
Database of American adults 127
Databases 83-85, 92
Databasic.io website 41-43
DataRefuge 69-71, 152
Dataset, definition of 21
Datasets 11
criteria for determining quality of 27-29
federal 69-71
finding of 27-29
government 69-71
objectivity of 154
U.S. 69-71
using existing 27-29
Davis, Michelle R. 228
Davos World Economic Forum Annual Meeting 247
Dawson, Jan 173
Debit card usage 199-203
Debt data 127
Deep learning 191
Deletion of customer data 180
Democratic Audit UK 231
Demographic data 127-130
Denver Post 95
Department of Commerce, U.S. 178
Department of Urban Development, U.S. 178
Design and data visualizations 44-46
Design choices in visualizations 253
DesMarais, Christina 80
DeVaney, James 196
Diaries 139-141, 159
Diaries, transcription of 148
Digital assistants iv
Digital dossiers 195, 197, 198
Digital footprints 80, 81, 89-91, 193
Digital labor 204-207
Digital marketing 98-100
Digital privacy 55-57, 80-82, 98-100
Digital Security Commission Act of 2016 104
Digital spying 209
Digital surveillance 209
Digital tracks. *See* Digital footprints.
Digital Trends 108
Digital wearables 95-97. *See also* Fitbit, Digital wearables.
Digitization of future thinking 176
Diller, Phyllis 148, 159
Disaster relief and data donations 247
Discover 133, 134C
Discrimination 176-179
Disney Princesses 214
Display announcements 61
DistrictAdministration 224
DIY Art 41-43
DMA 109
DNA 92-94

Do not call lists 64
Dobbs, Richard 231
Dobo, Nichole 195, 196, 197
Dockterman, Eliana 137
Document transcription 139-141
Documents 159
Domain-specific vocabulary 25
Dopamine 137
Dot plot 44-46
Doward, Jamie 129
Driverless trucks 184-187
Drivers' working conditions 185
DuckDuckGo 55-57
Duncan, Geoff 108
Dwoskin, Elizabeth 200
Dwyer, Jim 153
Dynamic content 143
Dynamic pricing 210
dynamic pricing i

E
Echo by Amazon 89-91
Echo Look 86-88
eCommerce 62-64
EcoRegions 145
EdSurge 196
Education Commission of the States 196
Education Week 218, 224, 228
EduCon 2.0 195
Egyptian hieroglyphs 254
Eilperin, Juliet 153
Elected officials, communication with
    108-110
Election of 2016 127-130, 152
Election of 2012 36
Elections 34-37, 127-130, 152
Electronic documents 90
Electronic Frontier Foundation 67-68, 227,
    229
Electronic grid 82
Elephant Expedition 75, 135
Elevator pitches 61
Email "junk" 172
Email curation 172-175
Email encryption 56, 60
Email services 172
Emotion 39
Employee behavior after-hours 96
Employee monitoring 96
Employees and health insurance 95-97
Employer knowledge of health behaviors
    95-97
Encrypted data 104-107
Encryption 58-61, 104-107, 119, 257
Encryption and criminal activity 106
Encryption legislation 105
Encryption of email 56
Encryption software 104
Encryption, end-to-end 105-106

Encyclopedia, online 156
Encyclopedias 23
End of Term Presidential Harvest 152
End of Term Web Archive project 151, 153
End-to-end encryption 105-106
End-user license agreements (EULAs)
    124-126, 174
energy efficiency i
Engadget 86
English class iii, 24
Enhancing student success 195-198
Environmental science 159-169
Epton, Abraham 240
Equal Credit Opportunity Act 192
Equal Employment Opportunity
    Commission, U.S. (EEOC) 178
ESRI Tapestry 64
Essays ii
Ethical behavior. *See* Ethical data use.
Ethical data use v, 58-61, 60, 94, 202, 204-
    207, 213-249
    in journalism 234-236
    of nudging 232
EULAs. *See* End-user licensing agreements.
EuroGentest 92
Europe 121
European Union Directive on Data
    Protection of 1995 122
Europeon Union and privacy policy 120-123
Evaluating an argument 21
Executive Office of the President 177
exercise trackers i
Exter, Monty 224
ExtremeTech (ET) 201
Eye of Sauron 62-64

F
Facebook i, 63, 117, 119, 129, 130, 192, 199,
    214, 244
    and advertisements 127-128
    and privacy 116-119
    and quizzes 129, 215, 216
Facial recognition software 144
Fair Credit Reporting Act 192
"Fair and accurate" standard 235
Faircloth, Kelly 98
Fallibility of numbers iv
Families 74, 80
Family Educational Rights and Privacy Act
    (FERPA) 227
Farming practices 155
Farook, Syed Rizwan 114
Fashion advice 86-88
Fast Company 205, 247
Fast Company Design 86
FBI. *See* Federal Bureau of Investigation.
FCC. *See* Federal Communications
    Commission.
"Fear factor" and data 234-236

Federal agencies 151-154
Federal Bureau of Investigation (FBI) 90, 111-114, 90
Federal Communications Commission (FCC) 101-103
Federal data 69-71, 151-154
Federal documents 151-154
Federal officials 110
Federal government 108-110
Federal labor laws 204
Federal Trade Commission (FTC) 64, 177, 180, 181, 182, 193, 194, 200, 238
Feinstein, Senator Dianne 105
FERPA. *See* Family Educational Rights and Privacy Act.
Field guides 143
Field work 161
Field-specific vocabulary 25
Filter Bubble, The (book) 57
Firefox browser 61
Firewalls 244
Fitbit 83-85
Fitness trackers 83-85, 95-97
FLASH 228
Flint Water Crisis 240-242
Florida Keys 167
FOIA. *See* Freedom of Information Act.
Fold.It 167, 256
Fontichiaro, Kristin 86-88, 265
Food packaging and nudges 232
Forbes 87, 92, 96, 99, 117
Ford, Martin 185
Fortune 89, 177, 193
Founding Fathers 114
Fourth Amendment 111-115, 190
Franklin, Ben 207
Fredrickson, Leif 240
Free market 60
Freedom from unwarranted search 111-115
Freedom of Information Act (FOIA) 191, 226
Friends 80
FTC. *See* Federal Trade Commission.
Fung, Brian 101, 243
Funk, McKenzie 129
Future crimes 188
Future of work 204-207
Future Tense 177
Future thinking 176

G
GalaxyZoo.org 167
Gallagher, Kerry 228
Gallup polls 36
Game mentality 138
Gamification and citizen science 135-138
Gardening practices 155
Gebhart, Gennie 227
Gen X 116, 118
Gen Z 116-119

Generational differences 116-119
Genetic diseases 92-94
Genetic testing 93
Genomic sequencing 92-94
George Washington University Libraries 151
"Getting off the grid" 82
German government 103
Ghosh, Shona 173
Ghostery 55-57, 61
Gibbs, Alice 129
Gift cards 99
Gig economy 204-207
Gillman, Todd 235
Gilpin, Caroline Crossin 80
Global Pulse Big Data Initiative (United Nations) 247
Gmail 175
Goldstein, Jessica 98
GoodReads 227-229
Google Translate 144
Google 175, 192, 199-203, 237
Google G Suite 217
Google Home 88, 89
Google Inside Adwords 201
Google Privacy settings 203
Google Public Data Explorer 44-46
Google Sheets 46
Gornes, Amilcah 195-198
Government data 69-71, 151-154, 247-250
    access to 151-154
    finding of 154
Government documents 151-154
Government incentives and predictive policing 190
Government paternalism 230-233
Government Publishing Office, U.S. 151
Government trust 233
Government websites 151-154, 252
GPS devices 111
Grades 117
Graepel, Thore 129
Graphs i, 36, 44-46, 253
Grassegger, Hannes 129
Grassroots movements 70-71
Great Britain, area of 22
Greenberg, Andy 105
Greenblatt, Alan 117
Gregg, Michael 209
Grid, electronic 82
Griffin, Amy 134
Guardian, The 129, 185, 237
Guidance systems 184
Gullo, Karen 227
Gum, chewing 16
Gun ownership data 127
Guterres, Antonio 247

H

Habitat Network 145-147
Hacking 62-64, 84, 85
Hagemann, Ryan 105
Hakim, Danny 128
Handwriting and transcription 149
Harmon, Katherine 231
Harris, Mark 237
Harvard Business Review 177, 193, 248
Harvard University 92, 92
Harwood, Matthew 209
Hasenkopf, Chris 247
Hatmaker, Tyler 188
Headlines 26
Health and data donations 247
Healthcare 95-97, 122, 155
Health data 118
Health indicators 95-97
Health insurance 93-97
    and digital wearables 94-97
    and employees 95-97
    companies 93-94, 95-97
    denial of 97, 167
Heart rate 83, 84
Heat maps 191
Hechinger Report, The 196
Hess, Amanda 98-99
Heuristics 52
Hieroglyphs 254
Higgins, John K. 193
Hill, Kashmir 99
Hillenbrand, Katherine 241
Hillman, Keith 137
Hing, Geoff 240
Histogram 44-46
Historical documents 139-141
Hitler, Adolf 103
Hobbits 62
Hoelter, Lynette 9-16, 29, 265
Hoff, Tyler 83-85, 89-91, 101-103, 148-150, 172-175, 243-246, 265
Hogwarts 214
Holands, Gareth J. 232
Holt, Lester 89
Home ownership data 127
"How to Read a Privacy Policy" 126
Hovinga, Kelly 132-134, 135-138, 192-194, 265-266
HTTPS Everywhere 55-57
Huffington Post 81, 173, 205 209
Humanitarian aid and data donations 247
Humanities and citizen science 139-141
Hvistendahl, Mara 189
Hype 236

I

Identity theft 62-64, 257
Igloo making 156
IK-MAP 156-157

Illegal activity, recordings of 89-91
Illnesses 97
Images 159
In-store purchases 199-203
Incarceration statistics 176
Income data 127
Independent contractors 206
Independent researchers 249
Industry self-regulation 108-110
Infographics ii, iii, 17-19, 50-54, 253
    definition of 50-54
    as visual arguments 50-54
    assignments with 50-54
    arguments with 50-54
    assignments for 54
    design elements of 50-54
    hunt for poor examples of, 53
    rubrics for 50-54
Information density 38-40
Information literacy 20-23
Ingraham, Christopher 241
Inquiry-based research 22, 55-57, 75
Instagram ii, 116
Institute of Museum and Library Services ii
Insurance companies 192
Insurance Thought Leadership 177, 179
Insurance, vehicle 97
Integrity 235
Intellectual privacy 55-57
Interactive whiteboards (IWBs) 32-33
Intercept, The 172-173, 189
International Brotherhood of Teamsters 185
International data privacy 129
International privacy policy 121
Internet Archive 153, 175
Internet browsing history 101-103
Internet Explorer 61
Internet of Things 209, 237-238. See also Fitbit, Apple Home, Amazon Echo, Google Home, Digital assistants.
Internet Service Providers 101-103, 243-246
Internet-connected devices 83-85, 86-88, 111
Interpretation of genetic data 93
Interrogating statistics 20-23
Intervals 253
Inuit practices 157
Invasion of Iraq 234
Invasions of privacy 180-183
IP address 183
iPhone 90, 114
Iraq, U.S. invasion of 234
Isaac, Mike 173
ISPs. See Internet service providers.
It's Complicated (book) 57

J

Jackson, Abby 196
Japsen, Bruce 96

Jefferson (blogger username) 153
Jenne, Inc. 224
Jewish identification during Hitler era 103
Jezebel 98
Jingles 16
Joint Resolution S. Res. 34. 244
Joke files 159
Joke files and transcription 148
Jones v. United States 111
Joque, Justin 38-40, 47-49, 266
Journalism and ethics 234-236
Journalistresource.org 224
Journals 46
Journals of physical activity 84
Journey North 256
Judges 176
Junk food and nudges 231
Junk mail 172-175
Just Security (website) 105
just-in-time interventions ii

K
Kalia, Amul 227
Kalanick, Travis 172
Kastrenakes, Jacob 101
Katz vs. the United States 111
Katz, Charles 111
Kavanaugh, Shane Dixon 189
KeePass 61
Kelley-Mudie, Sara 22
Kerr, Orin 112
Kestler-D'amours, Jillian 156, 157
Keys 254
Kharpul, Arjun 112
Kille, Leighton W. 224
Kindle 261
Klosowski, Thorin 173
Knorr, Caroline 80
Kofman, Ava 189
Kosaka, Glen 108
Kosinski, Michal 129
Krogerus, Mikael 129
Kudialis, Chris 224
Kumar, Neeraj 143

L
Lab documents iv
Labels 46, 254
LaChance, Naomi 112
Language indicators and data 24-26
Large-scale data collection 159-169
Larson, Quincy 244
Larson, Selena 86
Las Vegas Sun 224
Lasers 184
LastPass 61
Lead poisoning 240-242
Lead Safe Illinois 241
Lead testing 240-242

Leaf changes 167
Leaf identification 142-144
Leafsnap app 142-144
Learning analytics 51, 195-198
Learning standards. *See* standards.
Legal norms 155
Legislators 63
Lennex, Amy 266
Letter-writing campaigns 108-110
Letters 139-141, 159
Libertarian paternalism 230
Liberty 113
Library book circulation 217
Library of Congress 109, 151
Life events and privacy 98-100
Lifehacker 173
Lifestyle data 127
Likes 119
Line chart 44-46
LinkedIn 63
Loans 192-194
Location tracking 84
Logbooks 139
Lohr, Steve 173, 237
London School of Economics and Political Science 231
Londonderry School District 32-33
Long-haul trucking 184-187
Look (device) 86-88
Lord of the Rings, The 62
Los Angeles Times 200
Loyalty cards 63
Lyft 172

M
Machkovech, Sam 84
Macomb Community College 195
Magazines 46
Magid, Larry 228
Maheshwari, Sapna 181
Mainstream media 234-236
Manipulating data 36
    in spreadsheets 43
Mantha, Amurag 241
Manyika, James 231
Map of student data privacy 219
Mapmaking 145-147
Maps 35, 36, 38-40, 47-49, 156, 253, 254
    as data visualizations 39
    misleading 49
Margin of error 13-16
Marketing 199-203, 237
Marlinspike, Moxie 105, 106
Marshall, Jack 214
Marteau, Theresa M. 232
Martin, Alan 96
Marx, Eric 143
Maryland 160
Mashable 99

Math class i, 11
Matias, J. Nathan 205
Matsakis, Louise 205
Maximino, Martin 224
McCaul Commission 105, 107
McKenna, Sorcha 231
McKinsey Report 231
McLaughlin, Elliott 238
McSweeny, Terrell 193
Mean 9-12, 251
Mechanical Turk 204-207
Media 21
    bias in 35
Median 9-12, 251
Mele, Christopher 89
Metadata 58-61, 102
Meyer, Chelsey 133
Michigan 74, 162, 195
    wildlife of 74, 162
Michigan Zoomin 74, 135, 162
Microsoft 249
Microsoft Excel iii, 43, 46
Middle Earth 62
Millennials 116, 118
Millennium Bug 234
Mind the GAP strategy 17-19
Minds & Machines 248
Mini-lessons ii, 9-16
Minimum wage 204
Minority Report (movie) 188
Mobile computing and democratization 144
Mode 9-12, 251
Moeller, Susan 235
Monitoring of online behavior 62-64
Montana, Western 135
Mooney, Chris 153
Moorhead, Patrick 87
Morrison, Nick 117
Mortage lending industry 192-194
mortgages i, 194
Mosquito documentation 159
Motley Fool 96
MReport 193
Mullin, Kaitlyn 156
Murder investigation and Amazon Echo 89-91
Murnane, Kevin 117
Museums 141
Music preference data 128-129
My Congressional District tool (U.S. Census) 49

N

NASA. *See* National Aeronautics and Space Administration.
National Academy of Sciences 129
National Aeronautics and Space Administration 154
National Commission on Security and Technology Challenges 107
National Conference of State Legislatures (NCSL) 109
National Human Genome Research Institute (NHGRI) 92
National Institute of Justice 189
National Oceanic and Atmospheric Administration (NOAA) 154, 156
National Public Radio (NPR) 90, 102, 112, 117, 232
National Wildlife Federation 146
Native knowledge 155-158
Native plants 142-144, 145
Natural History Museum in London 142
Nature Conservancy 145, 146
Nature's cycles 167
NBC News 89, 121
NCSL. *See* National Conference of State Legislatures.
NEAToday 225
Negative correlation 13-16
Neighborhood associations 63
New Inquiry 206
New York 142
New York Times 57, 80, 89, 98-99, 120, 121, 128, 129, 153, 156, 157, 173, 174, 181, 217, 231, 237, 243
News media 34-37, 40, 46. *See also* Media, Newspapers
NewsDeeply 156
Newsletters 12
Next Generation Science Standards 259
Ng, Yin-Lam 232
Niskanen Center 105, 107
Nissenbaum, Helen Fay 57
NOAA. *See* National Oceanic and Atmospheric Administration.
Norms 155, 210
Northeastern United States 142
Not-for-profit partners 74
Nova Labs 167
Noyes, Katherine 177, 193
NPR. *See* National Public Radio.
Nudges 230-233

O

O'Connor, Anahad 231
Obama, Barack 36, 103, 153, 178
Obesity 231, 232
Obfuscation (book) 57
Oblivion 121
Obscurity 62-64
OCEAN theory of personality 130
Ocean Today 156
Ockdehal, Carina 186
Oehrli, Jo Angela 176-179, 266-267
Ohlhausen, Maureen 193
"OK, Google" 237
Old Farmer's Almanac, The 157

Old wives' tales 156, 158
Oliver, Adam 231
Olson, Parmy 96
On the Media 236
Online advertisements 199-203, 214, 215
Online information 176
Online marketing 98-100
Online payments 118
Online portals iv
Online privacy 101-103, 214-216, 243-246
Online quizzes and marketing 214-216
Online tracking 55-57
op-ed page iii
Open data 247-250
Open Government Act (proposed) 152
OpenAQ.com 247
Opera browser 60
Opportunity Project 179
Opsahl, Kurt 117
Opt-in programs 183, 215
Opt-out policies 103, 211
Oral Roberts University 83-85
Oregon 167
Otto 184
Outlier, definition of 251

P
"Packaging" existing data 249
Pacific Islanders 155
Pai, Ajit 101
Palo Alto, California 230
Pandora music app 128-129
Parent Coalition for Student Privacy 220
Parent-teacher conferences 74
Pariser, Eli 57
Parks, Jeffrey 241
Passive information gathering 86-88
Password managers 61
Password practices and behaviors 58-61
Pattern recognition 135-138
Pawelke, Andreas 248
"Paying" for free services 172-175
PBS. *See* Public Broadcasting System.
PC World 214
Penguin Watch 75, 135
Percent 9-12
Percent change 9-12
Percentiles 9-12
Performance expectation and bias 198
Permissions 58-61
Personal data ii, iv, v, 79-130, 246, 256-257
    management of ii, iv, v, 79-130, 246
    protection of 88
    hacking of 84
    sale of 56-57
Personal privacy 55-57, 80-82, 98-100, 101-103
Personal profiles 192
Personal spending 203

Personalized advertising 63, 214
Peterbilt 184
Petrescu, Dragos C. 232
Petronzio, Matt 99
Pew Research Center 124, 125
Pfefferkorn, Riana 105, 106
Phone apps and privacy 59-61
Phone hacking 237
Photo identification projects in citizen science 135-138
Photos iv, 58-61
Photosynthesis 159
Physical activity, tracking of 83-85
Pie charts iii, 44-46, 253. *See also* Charts.
Plant identification. *See* Leaf identification.
PLOS One 232
Poitras, Laura 57
Police 89-91, 189-190
Policy, U.S. 120-123. *See also* Laws.
Political affiliation 130
Politicians 176
Polls 34-37
Pollinators 145
Polonski Vyacheslav 235
Popular Mechanics 143
Population Clock (U.S. Census) 49
Population, U.S. 22, 122, 252
Porrino, Christopher S. 181
Posters vs. infographics 50-54
Prediction of student failure 195-198
Predictive algorithms. See Algorithms.
Predictive analytics 195-198, 209
Predictive policing 188-191
Predition of purchasing behaviors 199-203
Pregnancy 98-100
Presentation formats 32
Presidential Election of 2016 34-37
Presidential approval ratings 36
Presidential Innovation Fellows 178
Presidential Transition of 2017 152
Primary source documents 139-141
Privacy 55-61, 64, 80-82, 89-91, 97, 98-100, 116-119
    and life events 98-100
    as commodity 98-100
    as luxury good 98-100
    breaches of 60
    definition of 55-57, 111-115
    expectations by generation 116-119
    expenses related to 98-100
    vs. obscurity 62-64
    vs. security 224
    concept of 55-57
    cost of 99
    features of 239
    intellectual 55-57
    invasion of 62-64
    laws 120-123, 237
    policies 119, 120-123, 124-126

practices 55-57, 58-61
protections 182
protections by using cash 98-100
reasonable expectation of 111-115
regulation 243-246
settings 60
tools for 55-57, 243-246
student 65-68
Privacy Basics (Facebook) 119
PrivacyCheck browser extension 124-125
Private information 256-257
Proceeding of the National Academy of Sciences 129
Professional learning iii
Professors 84
Profiles i. *See also* Social media.
Progress of Education Reform 196
Proprietary data 129
ProPublica 181
Prosocial Big Data projects iv
Protecting personal information online 55-57
Protein folding 167
Protocols 68
Protonmail.com 60
Proxies 194
Proxy servers 244
Pruitt, Kobie 228
PSAT test 221
Psychological data profiles 127-130
Psychology 137
Psychology and citizen science 135-138
Public Broadcasting Service (PBS) 167, 217, 223
Public safety and surveillance video 223-226
Public service announcements 61
PublicPolicyPolling.com 37
Publish or perish 206
Pwned activity 58-61

Q
Qualitative variables 32
Quantitative literacy 9-12
Quartz 244, 245
Question marks 26
QuickFacts (U.S. Census) 130

R
R (data tool) 43
Race and algorithms 88
Race, prediction of 130
Racial justice 189
Radia, Ryan 101
Ramaswarny, Sirdhar 201
Ramirez, Edith 193
Ranking of solutions 232
Raphael, JR 214
Rapp, David 224
Rate of unemployment 52

Rates 9-12
Raw data 27-29, 37, 47-49, 97
Re-identification of anonymous data 92
Reading Apprencticeship model 17-19
Reasonable expectation of privacy 111
Reasonable suspicion 190
"Recipe for an Infographic" article 54
Recode 173
Regulations vs. nudges 232
Religion Dispatches 84
Religious data 127
Report cards 12
Research practices 30-33
Residential neighborhoods 145-147
Restaurants and calorie labels 231
Right to be Forgotten Law 64, 122
Right to obscurity 62-64
Riley v. California 114
River Keeping 132, 133
Roadkill 132, 133
Roberts, Chief Justice John 114
Roberts, Jeff 89
Robinlinus.com (website) 59-60
Robotization of jobs 184-187
Romney, Mitt 36
Root, Jonathon 84
Ropeik, David 133, 134
Rouse, Margaret 121
Rules of thumb 31, 34-37, 39, 40, 44-46, 251-257
Russell, Sharman 133
Ryvola, Scott 186

S
SAE International 186
SAE International Standard J3016 186
Safari browser 61
Safe driving discounts 97
Sailor logbooks 139
Sale of personal browsing behavior 244
Sampling 13-16
Samuels, Christina A. 224
San Bernardino shooting 90, 112, 113
SAT test 220-222
Save Our Streams 160
Sawers, Corinne 231
SC Magazine 108
Scaffolding 53
Scalia, Justice Antonin 113
Schell, Justin 69-71, 267
Schneier, Bruce 209, 210
School broadcasts 16
Scholastic 224
School data 65-68
School fitness requirements 83-85
School reunions 63
Schrage, Michael 177
Schubert, Christian 232
Science fairs 74

Scientific American 74, 93, 167, 189, 209, 231
Scientific journals, transcription of 148
Scientific vs. traditional knowledge 155-158
Scistarter.com 72-72, 161, 163, 166, 167, 256
Scott, Mark 121
Secretary General of the United Nations 247
Security 62-64, 113, 224
Self-designed research 30-33
Self-driving trucks 184-187
Self-esteem 88
Self-fulfilling prophecies 198
Self-regulation in industry 109
Selling data 130, 172-175, 180-183
Selyukh, Alina 90, 102, 112
Semuels, Alana 186
Senate Joint Resolution 34 102
Senate, U.S. 102
Sense-making 38
Sensors 97, 184
Sentencing 176
Seroff, Jole 20-23, 58-61, 104-107, 111-115, 120-123, 180-183, 267
Service learning 73, 75, 160
Sexual orientation 130
Sheninger, Eric 81
Shopping cards 63
Shopping habits 118
SI. *See* Smithsonian Institution.
Sicklick, Jeremy 193
Sigdyal, Pradip 177
Significance 13-16
Significance, statistical. *See* Statistical significance.
Simpson, John M. 186
Singer, Natasha 121
Siomoto, Jean 186
Siri 91, 237
Slice Intelligence 172-175
Slide decks 51
Smart home devices 86-88, 89-91, 180-183, 237-239
    and criminal activity 89-91
Smart televisions 180-183
Smartphone apps and privacy 59-61
Smartwatches 91. *See also* Apple Watch
Smith, Aaron 125
Smith, Brian Walker 186
Smith, Craig S. 156
Smith, Eileen 232
Smith, Jack IV 189
Smith, Susan 50-54, 72-75, 116-119, 159-169, 188-191, 223-226, 227-229, 267-268
Smithsonian Institution 142, 143
    Digital Volunteers 148
    transcription project of 75, 148-150, 166, 256
Smoking 16, 96
Snapchat 116

Social Explorer 47-49
Social media 56, 63, 67, 80-82, 98-100, 116-119, 191, 208, 236
    and "fear factor" 236
    "clean up" of 82
    benefits and drawbacks of 81
Social networks 191
Social norms 155
Social science data 47-49
Social Security number 257
Social services, distribution of 190
Society of Automotive Engineers 186
Socioemotional learning 73
Soda nudges 232
Soft skills 73
Soil collection 167
Sotomayor, Justice Sonia 113
Spartharou, Angela 231
Special education students 223-226
Spreadsheets 41-43
Spying on Students report 67-68, 227
Stafford, Tom 137
Stakeholders 32
Stalking 208-211
Standardized testing 17-19, 220-222
Standards 17-19, 51, 72-75
Standards for the 21st-Century Learner 20-23, 259
Standards of beauty 87
Standards of fashion 87
Stanford Cyberlaw 186
Stanford University Libraries 151
Stanley, Jay 117
StartPage 55-57
Stat 134
State Student Privacy Law Compendium 66
Statistical benchmarks 10, 20-23, 52, 252.
Statistical comprehension iii
Statistical language 15
Statistical literacy iii, 9-12, 251
    vs. math class 9-12
Statistical reading 24-26
Statistical significance 13-16
Statistical storytelling 24-26
Statistical strategies iii
Statistics 20-23
    and data comprehension 261
    and language 9-12
    in context 24-26
    context for 20-23
    interrogation of 20-23
Steelberg, Tierney 44-46, 268
Steketee, Amy M. 224
Stempeck, Matt 248
Step tracking 83-85
Step-counting 84
Stephens, Wendy Steadman 27-29, 55-57, 95-97, 98-100, 127-130, 142-144, 204-207, 268

"Stepping stone reading" 21
Stillman, Janice 157
Stillwell, David 129
"Stop, look, and listen" metaphor i
Storm identification 159
Story elements 53
Story framing 50-54
Storytelling 155
Strategic plans, 32
Strategic Relations 157
Strauss, Valerie 221
Strickland, Eliza 133
Stroud, Matt 189
Student data 65-68, 83-85, 195-198, 217-219
    law regarding, 218
    and privacy 220-222, 227-229
    map of 219
    physical activity and 83-85
    protection of 217-219
Student privacy 65-68
    and cloud storage 227-229
    principles of 222
Student rankings 196
Students 32
    with disabilities 223-226
Stuit, Martha 34-37, 43, 269
Sudden Oak Death 167
Sugary beverage nudges 232
Sullivan, Bob 121
Sunna, Samantha 235
Supporting Librarians in Adding Data Literacy Skills to Information Literacy Instruction ii
Supreme Court 106, 111, 208-211
Surveillance video 223-226
Surveillance vs. security 62-64
Surveys, language used in 15
SWOT analysis 232
Synthesis 51

T

Taddeo, Mariarosaria 248
Tag-a-thon citizen science activity 74
Tagging in citizen science 132
Tanner, Adam 92
Taplinger, Susan 109
Targeted advertising 63, 128, 180-183, 192
Targeting individuals via Big Data 208-201
Taser 188
Tatevossian, Anoush R. 248
Taube, Aaron 201
Teacher expectations of students 195-198
TeachingWithData.org 241
TeachTheVote 224
Team CGK 118
Teamsters 185
TechCrunch 188
    techniques for 30-33
TechRadar 244

Telematics devices 97
Television 180-183
Terms of service 124-126, 175
"Terms of Service; Didn't Read" site 126
Test scores 16
Testing 17-19, 197
Tetris 136, 137
textbooks i
The Onion Router (Tor). *See* Tor.
Theorizing the Web conference 99
thermostats i
ThinkProgress 93, 98
Third-party access 215, 218
Third-party accounts at school 65-68
Third-party services 227-229
Third-party tools, approval of 227-229
Third-party vendors 227-229
Thompson, Fraser 231
Timberg, Craig 200
Time 80, 99, 137
Time ranges 36
Timelines 53
Timm, Alex 177, 179
Tolkein, J.R.R. 62
Tone 26
Toobin, Jeffrey 121
Top-down movements 70
Topic exploration 20-23
Tor 55-57, 99, 245, 246
Tourism 190
Towey, Maurren 156
Trackers, fitness. *See* Fitness trackers.
Tracking devices 111
Tracking of television viewing 180-183
Tracking software 180-183
Tracking, online 55-57
Traditional knowledge 155-158
Transcription tasks 204-207. *See also* Smithsonian Institution Transcription Center.
Translation services 207
Transparency and data 210
Transportation industry 184-187
Tree data 143
Triangulation of data 199
Trident gum 16
Truckers 184-187
Trucking industry 184-187
Trucks.com 186
Trump, Donald J. 36, 37, 101, 103, 128, 153
Tufekci, Zeynep 87, 88
Tufte, Edward 52
Turner, Karen 238
Turtle banding 132
Tutorials 61
Twitter 80, 87, 162
Twitter and public opinion 234

U

U.S. Congress. *See* Congress, U.S.
U.S. Constitution. *See* Constitution, U.S.
U.S. Department of Commerce. *See* Department of Commerce, U.S. 178
U.S. Department of Urban Development. *See* Department of Urban Development, U.S.
U.S. Equal Employment Opportunity Commission. *See* Equal Employment Opportunity Commission, U.S.
U.S. Government Publishing Office 151
U.S. invasion of Iraq 234
U.S. News and World Report 95, 97, 218
U.S. policy. *See* Policy, U.S.
U.S. Population. *See* Population, U.S.
U.S. Senate. *See* Senate, U.S. 102
U.S. Supreme Court. *See* Supreme Court, U.S.
Uber 172, 173, 186, 206
    and autonomous vehicles 186
Unemployment rate 52
    calculation of 52
Unintentional consequences iv
United Kingdom 234
United Nations 247, 248
United Nations Global Pulse 248
United States Census. *See* Census, U.S.
United States v. Jones 113
United States v. Wurie 114
United States, area of 22
United States, Northeastern region 142
United States, population of 22
University of North Texas Libraries 151
University of Maryland 143
University of Michigan 74, 197, 198
University of Oklahoma 167
University of Texas at Austin 124
University of Washington 167
Unreasonable search 111-115
Unroll.me 172-175
Unwarranted search 112
Urban tree diversity 143
Urban wildlife 145-147
USA Phenology Network 167
USA.gov 64
Usable Privacy Policy Project 125
USAFacts.org 249
User agreements 124-126
User data, selling of 172-175
User profiles 192
User-added content 142-144

V

Variables 9-12
    qualitative 32
Vehicle insurance 97
Vehicle monitoring devices 95-97
Venmo 118
Venn Diagram 59

Verge, The 101, 189, 191
Vertesi, Janet 98-100
Vice 129
Video cameras 184
    and legislation 224
    and police 188-191
Video games and violence 22, 234
Views from Oxford 235
Violence and video games 22, 234
Viotty, Samantha 41-43, 269
Virtual Private Networks (VPNs) 59-61, 243, 244
Visual arguments 50-54
Visual design in infographics 50-54
VIsualDNA 215
Visualizations. *See* data visualizations.
Vizio 180-183
Vizio Smart TV 181
Vocabulary 25
Vocativ 189
Voice mail 90
Voice-activated technology 89-91
Volunpeers 148
Volvo 184
Voter data 127-130
Voters, number of 22
voting ii, 22, 34-37, 127-130
    and data literacy 34-37
    history data 127
Voyeurism 62-64
VPNs. *See* Virtual Private Networks.
Vulnerable populations 208-211

W

Waffle charts 44-46. *See also* Charts.
Wake words 90
Wakefield, Jane 215
Walker, Tim 225
Wall Street Journal 105
Wall Street Journal blog 214, 215
Wareable 96
Warrants for search 111
Washington Post 49, 101, 112, 153, 200-201, 202, 221, 238, 241, 243, 245
Washington Times 83
Washington, D.C. 110, 142
Watchdog groups 235
Water sampling 240-242
Water use data 90
Wax seals 104
Wayback Machine 69-71, 153
Weapons of mass destruction 235
Wearables. *See* Fitbit, Digital wearables.
Weather data iv
Weather prediction 155
Web traffic 243-246
Webinars 8-75
Weiner, Gabriel 186
Wen, Shawn 206

Western explorers 155
Wexler, Richard 209
Whatis.com 121
Whitarn, Ryan 201
White collar crime 189, 191
Whiteboards, interactive 32-33
WiFi, capturing of pings 211
WikiLeaks 237
Wikipedia 167
Wildlife 72-75
    of Michigan 162
    habitat fragmentation 146
    photography of iv, 72-75
Wildlife Society 146
Wildwatch Kenya 75, 135, 137
Williams, Connie 50-54, 72-75, 139-141,
    151-154, 155-158, 159-169, 269
Winston, Joel 92
Wired 105, 106
Wiretap Act 102
Woetzel, Jonathan 31
Wolff, Josephine 244, 245
Wolves 135
Women and artificial intelligence devices 87
Women and fashion tracking devices 87
WordCounter tool 41-43
Work and gender 204-207
Working conditions for drivers 185
Workplace privacy 95-97
World War II 121
Wright Law PLC Blog 186
Wright, Andy 148
Wright, Matthew 186
Writearounds 22, 40
WTF Visualizations site 40
Wu, Frank 173

X
x-axis 253

Y
y-axis 253
Y2K computer flaw 234
Yale Global Online 235
Yale University Library 235
YALSA Blog 143
YardMap project 145
Yellowstone National Park 135
"You are the product" 174
Young Adult Library Services Organization
    (YALSA) 143
YouTube 103, 105

Z
Zimmer, Carl 93
ZIP codes 145
Zooniverse.org 72-75, 135-138, 139-141,
    161, 163, 166, 167, 256